# The Telemachus Complex

*To my children, Tommaso and Camilla,*
*to their kingdom*


*'The smell of my son is as the smell of a field'*
*Genesis 27: 27*

Massimo Recalcati

# The Telemachus Complex

Parents and Children after the
Decline of the Father

Translated by Alice Kilgarriff

polity

First published in Italian as *Il complesso di Telemaco* © Giangiacomo Feltrinelli Editore Milano, 2013. All rights reserved.

This English edition © Polity Press, 2019

Polity Press
65 Bridge Street
Cambridge CB2 1UR, UK

Polity Press
101 Station Landing
Suite 300
Medford, MA 02155, USA

ISBN-13: 978-1-5095-3171-4
ISBN-13: 978-1-5095-3172-1 (pb)

A catalogue record for this book is available from the British Library.

Library of Congress Cataloging-in-Publication Data
Names: Recalcati, Massimo, auhor.
Title: The Telemachus complex : parents and children after the decline of the father / Massimo Recalcati.
Other titles: Complesso di Telemaco. English
Description: English edition. | Medford, MA : Polity, 2019. | Includes index.
Identifiers: LCCN 2019003896 (print) | LCCN 2019012784 (ebook) | ISBN 9781509531745 (Epub) | ISBN 9781509531714 (hardback) | ISBN 9781509531721 (pbk.)
Subjects: LCSH: Parent and child. | Father and child.
Classification: LCC BF723.P25 (ebook) | LCC BF723.P25 R4313 2019 (print) | DDC 306.874/2--dc23
LC record available at https://lccn.loc.gov/2019003896

Typeset in 12 on 15 pt Fournier MT by
Servis Filmsetting Ltd, Stockport, Cheshire
Printed and bound in Great Britain by TJ International Limited

The publisher has used its best endeavours to ensure that the URLs for external websites referred to in this book are correct and active at the time of going to press. However, the publisher has no responsibility for the websites and can make no guarantee that a site will remain live or that the content is or will remain appropriate.

Every effort has been made to trace all copyright holders, but if any have been overlooked the publisher will be pleased to include any necessary credits in any subsequent reprint or edition.

For further information on Polity, visit our website:
politybooks.com

# Contents

# Contents

# Introduction

> If men could have anything for the asking
> my first wish would be my *father's* return
> Homer, *Odyssey*, Book XVI

What I call the 'Telemachus complex' tackles the new forms of discontent affecting younger generations in an attempt to provide a new interpretation of the relationship between children and their parents at a time – such as ours – in which the symbolic authority of the father has lost its power, has been eclipsed, has faded irreversibly, as Eugenio Scalfari noted in an article written over fifteen years ago and fittingly entitled 'The Missing Father of Our Society'.[1] The difficulty faced by fathers in sustaining their own educational role and the intergenerational conflict that stems from this have long been noted, and not just by psychoanalysts. Fathers have gone missing, or have become their children's playmates. However, increasingly pressing signs are emerging from both civil society and the political and cultural worlds suggesting a *new and urgent demand for a father*. Just to be clear: it is my view that this eclipse does not indicate a provisional crisis of the paternal function destined to leave space for its eventual recovery. Addressing once more the theme of the decline of the paternal *imago* does not mean mourning the myth of the father-as-master. I personally harbour no nostalgia for the paterfamilias. His time has passed; it is over. The problem is not, therefore, how to restore the ancient and lost symbolic authority, but rather to examine what is left of the father after his dissolution. This is what interests me. In this context, I see the figure of Telemachus as a light in the darkness. He demonstrates the impossibility of separating the movement of inheritance (a singular movement and not an acquisition as a given right) from the recognition of being someone's child. Without this recognition, no symbolic filiation is possible.

The Telemachus complex is a reversal of the Oedipus complex. Oedipus viewed his own father as a rival, as an obstacle standing in his way. His crimes are the worst a human can commit: to kill one's father and sexually possess one's mother. The shadow of guilt falls on him and leads him to commit that extreme gesture of gouging out his own eyes. Telemachus, on the contrary, uses his eyes to scrutinize the sea, to watch the horizon. He waits for his father's ship to return, and for this father he has never known to restore the Law to his island now dominated by the Proci, his mother's suitors, who have occupied his home and are wildly plundering his property. Telemachus is emancipated from Oedipus' parricidal violence. He looks to his father not as a rival to fight to the death, but as a wish, a hope, as the possibility of reinstating the Law of the word in his land. If Oedipus embodies the tragedy of the *transgression of the Law*, Telemachus embodies that of the *invocation of the Law*. He prays for his father to return from the sea, placing in his return the hope that true justice is still possible in Ithaca. Whilst Oedipus' gaze is extinguished through the impotent fury of self-blinding as an indelible mark of guilt, Telemachus' gaze turns to the horizon to see if anything is returning from the sea. Of course, Telemachus risks falling into the trap of melancholy, of nostalgia for a glorious father, the king of Ithaca, the great hero who conquered Troy. The demand for a father, as Nietzsche well understood, always conceals the threat of an infinite, melancholic longing for someone who will never arrive. The risk taken by Telemachus is not unlike that of one of the two vagabonds in Samuel Beckett's *Waiting for Godot*. We already know that Godot is the name of an absence. No God/Father can save us: the nostalgia for the father as a hero is an unshake-able illness. The time of the father's glorious return has been left behind for good! No monuments, no invincible fleets, no party heads, no authoritarian and charismatic leaders, no gods or popes will return from the sea; only fragments, splintered pieces, fragile and vulnerable fathers, poets, directors, teachers with no job security, migrants, workers, simple witnesses who bear testament and demonstrate how to communicate a sense of faith in the future to one's own children and the new generations, giving a meaning to the horizon, a responsibility that does not lay claim to any notion of property.

We are in the era of the irreversible decline of the father, but we are also in the *era of Telemachus*. The new generations watch the sea, waiting for something of the father to return. But this wait is not a melancholic paralysis. The new genera-tions are involved, much like Telemachus, in performing that singular movement of recapturing their own future, their own inheritance. Of course, Homer's Telemachus waits to see the glorious sails of his heroic father's victorious fleet emerge onto the horizon. Yet all he finds of his father are the remains of a nationless migrant. At play in the Telemachus complex is not the demand to restore the father-as-master to his lost sovereignty. The demand for a father, which today marks the distress affecting the younger generations, is not a demand for power or discipline, but for *testimony*. We no longer have fathers-as-masters, only the need for fathers-as-witnesses. The demand for a father is no longer a demand for ideal role models, for dogma, for legendary, invincible heroes, for intransigent hierarchies, or an authority that is simply repressive and disciplinary. Instead it is a demand for acts, choices, passions that can bear witness to how we can exist in this world with both desire and responsibility. The father invoked today can no longer be the father who has the final word on life or death, or on the meaning of good and evil; he can only be a father who is radically humanized, vulnerable, incapable of revealing the meaning of life but capable of demonstrating, *through the testimony of his own life, that life can have a meaning*.

We have all been Telemachus. We have all, at least once, stared at the sea waiting for it to return something to us. And we could add, as Mario Perrotta does in his intense theatrical restaging of the *Odyssey*, that 'something always returns from the sea'.[2] Yet, unlike Telemachus, we are not the children of Odysseus. We will not inherit a kingdom. We are not princes awaiting the return of their father-king. If Telemachus, as we

4

will see in this book, shows us the right way to inherit, the condition of today's young Telemachus is one of disinheritance: lack of future, destruction of experience, loss of desire and enslavement to deadly enjoyment, unemployment and job insecurity. Do our children populate the dark 'night of the Proci'?[3] What kind of father will be able to save them if our time is that of his irreversible decline? Our children will not inherit a kingdom, but a dead body, a broken country, a crazed economy, unlimited debt, a lack of work and of a vital horizon. Our children are exhausted. So how, as I attempt to demonstrate in this book, can Telemachus be the paradigm for their position in this world? Why Telemachus and not Oedipus, with his rabid fight to the death with his father? What makes Telemachus the highest and most just Anti-Oedipus? He is neither a victim of his father, nor does he side stubbornly against his father. Telemachus is the rightful heir, he is the rightful son. 'He is not just a young man looking for his father, but a young man who needs a father. Telemachus is the icon of the son.'[4] This is a central premise of both this book and that which I will call the 'Telemachus complex'. Oedipus cannot be a son and Narcissus suffers the same fate. These two figures of classical mythology were chosen by Freud and by psychoanalysis as paradigmatic characters in the theatre of the unconscious. But neither accesses the generative dimension of the heir that is implicit in being someone's child. Oedipus remains a prisoner of his hate dressed up as love for his father (the father as an Ideal and the father as a rival constitute the two poles of the oscillation typical of what Freud refers to as the 'Oedipus complex'), whereas Narcissus is unable to separate himself from his own idealized image, and his fascination with this leads him to suicide. Rivalry (Oedipus) and autistic isolation (Narcissus) impede the singular movement of inheritance, without which any symbolic filiation is missing, alongside, as a consequence, the transmission of desire from one generation to another.

What struck me as most positive during the recent student protests were the 'book-shields'.[5] They were enormous, man-sized books, made out of foam and cardboard with a wooden centre, and painted in various colours. In the middle they carried the book's title and the name of its author. What wonderful shields, I thought! The military motif of defence against the aggressor is outclassed by the invocation of Culture – the Law of the word – as a barrier against the unjust violence of the economic crisis. I would be interested to learn more about the books that were chosen, a discovery that would no doubt be full of surprises. But the knowledge that certain books had been included (such as *The Odyssey*, *The Aeneid* and *The Italian Constitution*) has already comforted me in my conviction. What are these book-shields if not an invocation of the father? What, if not an invocation of the Law of the word as the Law of desire? It is, of course, an invocation that goes beyond the registry office, beyond blood or ancestry. Whilst, nowadays, the book as an object risks being transformed into an anonymous file, and bookshops, where it was so wonderful to lose oneself, turned into sets from waxwork museums of the twentieth century, these young people, using their book-shields, invoke their right to be heretical heirs, to be heirs in the right way. This is the thesis in this book to which I am most strongly wedded: the heir is always an orphan, always without inheritance, disinherited, uprooted, with no patrimony, left by the wayside, lost. Inheritance is never a simple pouring out of riches or genes from one generation to another. Inheritance is not a naturally sanctioned right, but a singular movement with no guarantees, leading us to our unconscious matrix. It is the taking-forward of that which we have always been. It is, as Kierkegaard would say, 'retreating advance'. This all takes place against the backdrop of an impossibility. No father can actually save us, no father can spare us the dangerous journey that offers no guarantee of inheritance.

Today, children seem to be devoid of any inheritance; they seem to have been consigned to an impossible inheritance. But do we not always inherit the impossible? Do we not always inherit a dead body? Inheritance never fills the void opened in the structural absence of the Father, but it always and only ever provides a way to cross it. Nevertheless, the passing down of a gift that can humanize life is always at play when it comes to inheritance. How can this gift be passed down at a time when the older generations have severed ties with the new, having given up the responsibility of their word? At a time when the gift that can humanize life is no longer guaranteed by the existence of the big Other of tradition? This Other has revealed itself to be what it has always been – inconsistent. If the new generations do not receive the gift from traditional fathers, then the gift can only be passed down through an encounter with testimony. So what is at play, then, when testimony is the gift? The gift that humanizes life is nothing more than the gift of desire and its Law. This is the only real kingdom that can be passed from one generation to the next. How can the *human humus* be made fertile? [6] How can the vital power of desire be passed down through the chain of generations? How can we structure an efficient process of symbolic filiation? The Telemachus complex articulates itself around these questions. Telemachus is the rightful heir, not because he inherits a kingdom, but because he reveals to us that it is only through the transmission of the Law of desire that life can emancipate itself from the deadly seduction of the 'night of the Proci', from the mirage of a freedom reduced to pure will of enjoyment. The *human humus* needs this Law to be generative.

Milan, December 2012

I

# The Law of the Word and the New Hell

## Praying Is No Longer Like Breathing

There was a time when praying was like breathing, when praying was a force of nature. Prayer had the same force as snow, rain, sun, fog. It was like the passing of the seasons: it was a collective ritual that articulated our daily life. I cannot remember when I learnt to pray. It is as if I have always known how. I was taught to pray in the same way I was taught to show respect for my elders and to behave at the table. I grew up at a time when praying was like eating, sleeping, running. That time, when praying was comparable to a force of nature, to breathing, has definitively come to an end. We are now in another time, one in which parents must, for example, choose whether or not to pass on the meaning of prayer to their children. If praying is no longer a practice that is passed on automatically through the force of tradition, if this is no longer a mechanism whose ability to function is guaranteed by the symbolic power of the Other, then the time of prayer has become the time of a subjective choice. Parents are obliged to make a conscious decision, one that is no longer automatically passed down through the Other of tradition.

At the beginning of *Cosa resta del padre?* [*What Remains of the Father?*],[1] I ask whether in the time of the death of God – the epochal event that defines the horizon of our time – it still makes sense to teach our children to pray. Some of my fellow psychoanalysts were eager to remind me that psychoanalysis had closed off all contact with religious discourse, and that my reasoning oscillated ambiguously between the risk of a nostalgic exhumation of the father's body, or that of God himself. As if asking questions about the meaning of prayer necessarily meant the nostalgic evocation of a religious society founded on the symbolic authority of the God-as-father.

## Aphonia and the Father's Amnesia

I have previously described the time we live in using a formula belonging to Lacan: that of *the evaporation of the father*.[2] I did not use this expression simply to comment on the crisis faced by real fathers in exercising their authority, but, more radically, to expose the failure of the guiding function of the Ideal in individual and collective life. More precisely, this formula demonstrates how it is impossible for the father to still have the final word on the meaning of life and death, on the meaning of good and evil. This word retreats, extinguishes itself; it appears worn out, exhausted. This word no longer exists. This point is demonstrated with great lyrical force in the opening scene of Nanni Moretti's 2011 film *Habemus papam*. The balcony of St Peter's stands desperately empty. Moretti knowingly lingers on the movement of the purple curtains fluttering in the wind, which, rather than announcing the presence of a new pontiff, instead reveal to the faithful, who stand in trepid anticipation, the melancholy and definitive absence of their beloved father. He who has been named by the College of Cardinals as a symbol of God on Earth, as the unique representative of His word, is not up to the task of carrying the symbolic weight of the role. His word falters, it is extinguished. He remains silent. It is something more than a humanization of the heir of St Peter, as film critics chose to see it. What Moretti is showing us is the evaporation of the father as an impossibility of carrying the symbolic weight of a word that still wishes to proclaim the ultimate meaning of the world, that of good and evil, of life and death. It is the breakdown of the time in which praying was like breathing. The new pope's aspiration to be an actor, his frustrated theatrical vocation, reveals how the word of the father has now been reduced to mere semblance. A game, fiction, betrayal, illusion, recitation, *mise en scène*. When, on the balcony of St Peter's, the new pope must speak in his symbolic capacity of Father to the faithful, his voice can no longer recite his part. It remains aphonic, aphasic; he withdraws into silence.[3] The word does not want to come out, it does not take shape, remaining trapped beyond the voice, revealing the aphonia, aphasia of the Father-pope, of the universal symbol of the father. Is this aphasia not one of the fundamental symptoms of our time? The multitude of souls that fills St Peter's Square awaiting the guiding words of the father are left disappointed, bewildered. The very person who should have offered them reassurance, who should have brought them encouragement, who should fill existence on Earth with the power of the word of God, is not only incapable of speaking, but reveals himself to also be lost. With a masterstroke, Moretti hits a nerve, suddenly inverting the generational order. The father who should reassure must now be reassured himself; the father who saves (us) from getting lost is lost himself. The father who should save his own children himself becomes a child. Generational metamorphosis: the Father-pope has become a terrified and crying child, who must be consoled and protected. An infantilization of the powerful adult image of the great paterfamilias. Generational inversion: who is the father? Who is the child? Who is offering shelter? Who is lost?

This scene from *Habemus papam* evokes another (equally pertinent) scene from Moretti's work, which is well worth revisiting. I am referring to *Palombella rossa*, the film shot by Moretti in the aftermath of the crisis in the Italian Communist Party (PCI) and the fall of the Berlin Wall, released in 1989. Faced with questions from a television journalist on the fate of the party, the secretary of the PCI, the film's protagonist played by Moretti, hesitates, appearing disoriented to the point of losing his memory. Rather than answering the journalist's questions, he asks himself: who am I? Who are we? What has happened? Here we find ourselves faced with another symptom, one with which the psychoanalyst is all too familiar: amnesia. This corresponds with and is, in some ways, fatally evoked by the aphonia-aphasia of the Father-pope. Who am I? Who are we? What has happened? The party secretary is no longer able to guide the party faithful. He is lost in the fog of a memory that has suddenly become unstable. Like the Father-pope, he is absent from himself. His memories plunge him into a series of sketches that hark back to his childhood: the smell of summer, the atmosphere in the swimming pool, the water polo matches, the ever-present bread and Nutella, *Doctor Zhivago*. The questioning about the collective destiny of the party leads to a dramatic calling into question of its very existence. Who am 'I'? Where am I? Where am I from? Where am I going? The metaphysics of the question outclasses that of the response.

At the intersection between *Habemus papam* and *Palombella rossa*, the two great symbols of the Ideals that have guided the lives of the masses in the West (the leader of the Holy Roman Catholic Church and the secretary of the glorious Communist Party) are no longer able to speak, they can no longer carry the symbolic weight of their public role. They appear lost, evaporated.

## The Hell of Salò

One final cinematographic reference can provide an even more radical summary of the phenomenon of the father's evaporation and its effect on our time. I refer to the last film-testament of Pier Paolo Pasolini: *Salò, or the 120 Days of Sodom*. Pasolini wilfully conceived this as a film that is impossible to watch. This is common in the most extreme contemporary art: the unveiled real of what is terrifying forces the spectator to retreat into anxiety. The horror of what is shown onscreen forces the spectator to lower their eyes, rendering the gaze impossible, as happens in one of the final scenes, in which a victim is sodomized whilst being brutally scalped with a knife, before being killed mercilessly.

Pasolini's final film wants to show the real of enjoyment without any symbolic filters: sadistic torture, coprophagia, humiliation, brutality, gratuitous murder. 'Everything is good when it is excessive', is the Bataille-esque statement made by one of the four sadistic libertines in the film's opening scene. The victims are presented as pure instruments at the service of the only Law of enjoyment: bodies are lacerated, throats are slit, they are tormented, burned, tortured and cynically murdered. In this Godless universe there is no salvation, there is no horizon, no desire. Everything is consumed in the claustrophobic compound of the will to enjoy. Though Pasolini had long used his works to promote a version of the sexual body, inspired by Rousseau and Bataille, as a transgressive force that challenges the repressive and coercive dimension of the Law in the name of the (impossible) return to Nature, in *Salò* he seems to move away from this representation of the conflict between the Law and desire, recognizing that the cult of enjoyment and the logic of its pure waste (present in Sade and theorized by Bataille) have become a rule for the biopolitical administration and manipulation of bodies under the new Law dictated by the capitalist discourse: compulsive sex, the assertion of a freedom without Law, the eternal repetition of all the Sadean scenarios demonstrate that our time has made enjoyment an imperative which, rather than liberating our lives, oppresses and enslaves them.[4] Herein lies the radical political indictment that runs through

*Salò*. It is in no way, as Cesare Musatti believed, an outburst of perverse-polymorphic sexuality faced with the failure of a normative access to a fully genital sexuality that would reveal the unconscious fantasy of its author,[5] but a rather more lofty attempt at describing the very unconscious of the capitalist discourse as a radical destruction of the Eros of desire.[6] It is in no way a depiction of a private theatre used to portray Pasolini's perverse fantasy (as a purely pathographical application of psychoanalysis to this film would do), but an exhibition of 'excess' as the assertion of a Law that rejects any limits and that qualifies the neo-capitalist degradation of the erotic body to a mere instrument of enjoyment. It is not a provocative representation of the polymorphic sexuality of childhood, but a desperate and entirely anti-erotic enjoyment that, without even the slightest regard for the Law of symbolic castration, melds disastrously with the death drive. Is this not one of the fundamental ciphers of our time, a time in which the command to enjoy seems to triumph as the only form of the Law?

Having only seen *Salò* once in my youth, in 1976, I had wrongly remembered a scene in which a boy and a girl, whilst being drowned in a bucket of shit, reacted to their imminent death one by making the sign of the cross, and the other by holding up a closed fist. Having recently watched Pasolini's film once more, I realized that this scene does not exist, but was the result of my unconscious combination of another two scenes in the film. In one of these, a girl finds herself immersed in shit and invokes the Christian God – 'God, God, why have you forsaken us?' – whilst in another scene, a soldier from

Salò is discovered as he makes love to a servant girl – thus transgressing the Law, which by insisting that there can only be enjoyment paradoxically prohibits the possibility of love – and is brutally riddled with bullets. Before dying he has time to proudly raise his closed fist. This 'error of memory', in reality, contains a subjective interpretation that I think remains incredibly faithful to Pasolini's narrative: the capitalist discourse drowns ideals (both Christian and communist) in shit and blood in the name of enjoyment, as the only paradoxically possible form of the Ideal and the Law. More precisely, Pasolini reaches Lacan when he demonstrates how, in perversion, the subject is chosen to placate a new God, a God who has absolute power over the Other, a God of enjoyment who decimates any sense of limit. Is this not perhaps the supreme ambition inhabited by the terrible quartet in Salò? Pasolini declares this explicitly in an interview on the Marquis de Sade with Gideon Bachmann and Donata Gallo, when he states that 'by using the bodies of their victims as things, the libertines are gods on Earth, their model is always God'.[7]

As with Moretti, in Pasolini's last film the symbols of Christianity and communism founder miserably. However, whilst Moretti draws attention to the psychological symptoms of our time (aphasia, amnesia), Pasolini illustrates in a Foucauldian sense the ontology of the body that implies these symptoms, or rather the perverse reduction of the body itself to a purely Sadean machine of enjoyment. For this reason, our time (as prophetically anticipated by *Salò*) is the time in which ideals are revealed to be inconsistent, apart from that of enjoyment (of death) as life's ultimate aim. 'Don't you know we would like to kill you a thousand times?', screams one of the torturers in the face of a terrorized victim. The machine of the capitalist discourse consumes itself infinitely, as occurs in the eternally repetitive and claustrophobic scenes depicted by the Marquis de Sade: their anonymous seriality demonstrates how enjoyment must always return to the same place in order to forestall the event of death.[8] The machine has to demonstrate that the only thing worth living for is one's own enjoyment, that no Law exists outside the one imposed by the command to enjoy. This is the profoundly perverse content in *Salò* and this is, most decisively, what is at stake in our time. What is worth living for? Is there a convincing response to this question, an alternative to the Sadean one? What I mean is: is there an ethical alternative to this logic, one that does not resort moralistically to either 'common sense' or the abstract universality of a Kantian practical reason? Does an ethical alternative exist that can *forcibly* oppose the affirmation of cynical enjoyment as the only value of life? Is this not a decisive question for our time, a time that promotes the enjoyment of the One as the earthly beatification of life? Is another future possible, one that is different from that predicted by the machine of the capitalist discourse, by the crazed machine of enjoyment? Is this not the answer that the new generations are waiting to hear from us? Does an Other enjoyment exist, different from that of the libertines depicted by Pasolini in *Salò*, and capable of making life worth living?

The weakening and the widespread crisis of the educational discourse give rise to the traumatic dimension of enjoyment unleashed by the Law of castration. It is the clinical theme I developed fully in my book *L'uomo senza inconscio* [*Man Without Unconscious*]: in the time of decline of the symbolic Other, of the foundering of the Ideal, of a defacing from which it can never recover, deadly enjoyment no longer seems capable of finding adequate symbolic barriers. If the Ideal once had the function of guiding enjoyment, differentiating itself from satisfaction, positively channelling the force of its drive, its decline seems to have left existence without a compass. Nevertheless, the practice of psychoanalysis cannot instigate the nostalgic recovery of the Ideal. This points, rather, to desire as the possibility of realizing (thanks to the Law of the word and the refusal of deadly enjoyment) a new, supplementary enjoyment, an enjoyment Other, an Other enjoyment as opposed to the deadly one Lacan defines using the term *surplus-jouissance* or *surplus-enjoyment.*[9] Something we ought to be aware of today is that the weakening of the normative action of the Symbolic has made transgression itself a conformist inclination of the drive. Enjoyment in and of itself is a radical form of the most reactionary spirit. Eternal love is much more transgressive than that which passes from one body to another without any amorous bond. The experience of remaining faithful to the Same is much more transgressive than the empty cult of the New. The appearance of modesty is much more transgressive than its extinction. Nothing, in fact, seems more likely to be considered obscene! The proliferation of enjoyment unleashed by the Law of the word demonstrates how the intervention of the Symbolic is no longer capable of tempering the real of enjoyment, which instead proliferates in a way that is limitless. The sentiment of the obscene implies, in fact, a belief in the limit, in the ethical value of modesty, whilst in the age of the triumph of the disenchanted cynic and narcissist, brought about by the affirmation of the capitalist discourse, this belief is destined to eclipse itself, causing our time to be one of excessive enjoyment, an era of trauma.[10]

## The Law of the Word

The terrifying drama of Pasolini's *Salò* is that which Lacan called *jouissance mortelle*, or deadly enjoyment. This is an enjoyment that respects no symbolic limit, a profoundly incestuous, and therefore deadly, enjoyment.[11] We find this form of enjoyment in the tale of Telemachus. Is the night of *Salò* not, in fact, like the 'night of the Proci', the night of enjoyment without desire, of enjoyment as a pure dissipation of life? The violation of bodies by the perverse quartet in Pasolini's *Salò* is the perfect continuation of the uninterrupted violation to which young princes submit the house of Odysseus, his son Telemachus and his wife Penelope in the *Odyssey*. This violation, this offence, breaks the only version of the Law that counts, from a psychoanalytic point of view. To which Law am I referring? To an unwritten Law, one that is absent from the legal Codes and Law books. A Law that cannot even be found in the biblical Decalogue, but which is the cornerstone of any possible Civilization, or rather, the very idea of Civilization itself. It is a Law that makes all other Laws possible. Psychoanalysis calls this fundamental Law the *symbolic Law of castration*, but we can also call it the *Law of the word*. What does this Law, which is a *Law of the laws*, establish? It establishes that as the human is a being of language, as its house is a house of language, its existence cannot help but manifest itself through the word. It establishes that the event of the word is what humanizes life and makes the power of desire possible by introducing the experience of loss to the human heart. What does this mean? It means that life is humanized and differentiated from animal life through its exposure to language and the act of the word. Purely biological life is mortified by the action of language. It cannot remain attached to the umbilical cord, or the breast, or its own faeces, and nor can it have everything, enjoy everything, be everything, just as one cannot talk whilst eating or subtract themselves from the bonds of communication between speaking-beings imposed by the laws of language, and so on. But this symbolic mortification is not an amputation of life (as the Sadean libertine and the paedophile, who search for enjoyment beyond language in the uncorrupted, innocent bodies of victims or the child, erroneously believe) but its greatest source of wealth. The experience of the impossible has a close relationship with the existence of language. It is language that acts as a structure of separation, imposing a loss of life on life as a condition of its humanization. This loss must not, however (let's say it again), be seen as a moral penance, a deficit or an illness. It is not a condemnation, a sacrifice or a theological curse. It is the salvation of life because only the encounter with the existence of the limit and the lack can generate desire as a generative force, deflecting it from the neurotic cult of sacrifice and perverse fanaticism for deadly enjoyment. Neuroses and perversion are, in fact, two names that indicate either a sacrificial adoration of the limit (neuroses), or an emphasis on enjoyment that rejects any experience of the limit (perversion). They are two false moves that generate only suffering and illness. Whilst neurotic inhibition cultivates a pathological passion for the limit with the aim of proving the existence of the Other as ideal (as a refuge and absolute guarantee of life), the perverse stages the limit, only to transgress it repeatedly, to deny the impossible, to make 'everything possible'.[12]

The experience of the limit is introduced by the Law of Castration as the Law that promises to save humankind from the abyss of deadly enjoyment. The Law that sustains desire as the possibility of reaching an Other enjoyment different from deadly enjoyment does not oppress life, but potentially liberates it. Is this not what happens in the relationship between children and their parents? On the one hand, the child will encounter in their parents the inassimilable kernel of the impossible, of the limit, of the Law as that which forbids the incestuous enjoyment of everything, but on the other, thanks precisely to the encounter with this impossible, the child will become an heir, they will receive the right to desire for themselves, they will receive the power of the Law of desire, the faculty that brings life to life.

More precisely, the Law of the word lays down the symbolic prohibition of incest: if the human being is a being of the word, this means that they are separated from the immediate enjoyment of the maternal Thing. This means that the Law of the word, castrating incestuous enjoyment, forbids, as Lucretius would say, 'everyone from wanting everything'. This introduces us to the dimension of life that is finite, dependent, damaged. It imposes the renunciation of immediate enjoyment and its fantasy of self-consistency. It ensures that the humanization of life entails a renunciation of the integral satisfaction of the drive. From this point of view, the Law of the word, the symbolic Law of castration, introduces an exchange that lies at the basis of every possible social pact: by renouncing the enjoyment of everything, of wanting everything, of being everything, of knowing everything, it becomes possible to have a Name, to be human, an inscription on the body of the community to which I belong. If I accept the loss of part of my being – if mankind (to quote Lucretius once more[13]) *'learn[s] to watch out for himself, his own will to survive'*, my existence will earn its human meaning, it will be able to give meaning to its presence in the world, it will be able to participate in the life of the city, have the right to citizenship in the community of speakers and mortals.

The event of the word is, first and foremost, the event of a symbolic cut that inscribes in the human the dimension of the impossible. Life that yields to the Law of the word is life that is impoverished, life mortified by the symbol, but it is, for this very reason, life that is open to life, life of desire, life that goes beyond nature, life immersed in the order of culture. If the Law of the word did not run through life, it would be a purely animalistic, headless drive, a tendency for the most immediate enjoyment, a life dominated by instinct, a life attached to life, with no mortal destination. The action of the Law of the word exposes life to the impossible, thus rendering it human. Because of the existence of the Other of language, human life is never its own master, but finds itself thrown into life without, as Heidegger would say, 'mastering its own foundations'. This means that human life can never be its own master. No speaking-being can create themselves, can consist only of themselves. No life can do without the Other of language. We cannot become absolute masters of our own lives. Rather, when life pursues the realization of this ideal of being master it always ends up in the lethal and totalitarian illusion that annihilates it in the very name of its assertion.[14]

The exposing of life to its limitless contingency generates the human as a thing that comes from the Other. More than anything, the Law of the word sanctions life's lack of foundation, separating it from itself, thus annihilating the identitary unity of pure animal life. Language acts on life revealing it to be never self-determined (not even by instinct) but constitutively dependent on the action of the Other. Without the presence of the Other human life dies, it withers, it loses the very sentiment of life, it switches itself off. This is clearly evidenced by childhood traumas linked to early abandonment. The Law of the word is the Law of recognition of the desire of the Other with which human life is nourished. In order for my existence to have meaning, in order for it to constitute itself as human, it requires not only bread but the yeast of desire of the Other. In this sense, the life of the *parlêtre* (*speaking-being*) is an appeal, a demand to love from the Other, a demand to be something for the desire of the Other. If this yeast is missing, life falls into nonsense, it becomes life without life, a spent life.

## How Do We Transmit the Word of the Law?

Life begins to die when we begin to speak, because it is the act of speaking that reveals how life is exposed without foundations to language and its Law, which is the Law of the Other. The father is the symbol of this Law and for this reason he is held to preserve the experience of the impossible above all else. If life is only humanized by the encounter with the prohibition of incest, the father can only carry out this inscription if he takes upon himself the event of the limit (the event of the impossible), demonstrating how he too is subject to the Law of the word. This means that a father is not he who possesses the final word on the meaning of life and death, but rather he who knows how to bring the word and, consequently, how to relinquish the power of having the final word. If a father does not take upon himself the experience of the impossible that the Law of the word inscribes in the human being, the Law would degenerate, becoming nothing more than a mere authoritarian imposition. If it does not want to simply reproduce a sadistic enacting of the Law, the act that introduces the impossible must be mediated by a unique testimony that takes on the very meaning of the limit. What I mean is that in order for the limit to have a symbolic function, the limit must, first and foremost, be experienced by the person who makes it exist. One example of this can be found in the biblical tale of the sacrifice of Isaac. What should really strike us most in this tale is not so much the sacrificial offering of Isaac to a bloodthirsty God, but Abraham's submission to the Law of the word, which demands that even his most beloved, long-awaited son, the son of promise, must be lost, must be abandoned. Abraham, the father, does not have the final word on his son's fate, but is the one who knows how to lose him, how to let him go. In this sense, he is not the Law but is responding to a Law (the Law of the word), which towers above him and forces all parents to lose their children, to let them go, to sacrifice enjoyment of their child, to not consider their children their own property. But we can also make reference to other examples. That of a father who, when faced with his anorexic daughter who has been hospitalized because she is dying and so must be force-fed, abandons his modest financial empire to spend his nights at her bedside. He renounces his own immediate enjoyment, made up of operations on the stock market, shares, acrobatic buying and selling, to move deeper into a different territory. His daughter will later describe this as the gesture of a 'knight who abandons his armour for love'. This man had always ensured his favourite daughter wanted for nothing, having diligently taken care of her after the death of his wife. Yet here for the first time he gives her the gift of his own lack, of his inadequacy as a father, the gift of his vulnerability. Finally he can give his daughter not that which he has (his 'animal feed' as she dismissively describes it), but that which he does not have, or rather, the sign of his lack.[15] In this way he renounces being the Law but, by applying the Law to himself, is able to liberate himself from that rigid armour that makes every one of his gestures seem cold, bureaucratic and anonymous. By encountering the Law of castration he can recognize how slavishly he identifies with an entirely sadistic Law. In this case, the anorexic blackmail (in its tragic mercilessness) forces him to dissolve that identification and recognize another Law, the Law of the word, which allows him to give his daughter his own castration, to reach her not through a limitless and anonymous stream of objects, but through the sign of love.

We find another two examples in cinema. The first is from the film *Billy Elliot* (2000), written by Lee Hall and directed by Stephen Daldry, in which a son's dream of being a ballet dancer, initially strongly opposed by his humble mining family because the image is so damaging to the virile image of the male in a group culture that is crude, chauvinist and homophobic (his father had unsuccessfully tried to push him into boxing), is finally supported unreservedly by the father and older brother when the tenacity of the boy's desire is made clear. At a time of great economic crisis for British mining in 1984, the father shoulders an incredibly heavy debt and subjective humiliation (breaking the strike of which he was one of the organizers) in order to be able, through the mobilization of an entire community, to offer his son the chance to take the entrance exams for a renowned ballet school.

But even more effective is the lesson taught by the Belgian film *The Son* (*Le fils*) (2002), by Jean-Pierre and Luc Dardenne, which tells the story of a boy who has murdered someone his own age, and who, upon leaving prison, is forced to undertake a period of re-education with a man who is in fact (unbeknownst to the boy) the father of the child he had killed, and who in order to reintegrate him into society, takes it upon himself to teach the boy carpentry. The boy goes through this re-educational process without even vaguely grasping the gravity of the act he has committed. For him the Law is merely an external limitation that imposes certain conditions on him for his reintegration into society. When the father discovers the identity of the boy who has been entrusted to him, he barely manages to control his thirst for revenge. After having discovered the identity of his mentor, the boy tries to escape but is recaptured by the man, who manages, at the very last minute, to stop himself from committing another homicidal act by strangling the boy. The Law of retaliation is suspended by the Law of the word. From here, from this father's submission to the Law, from his renunciation of the enjoyment of revenge, flows the possibility of a new and more authentic symbolic adoption of the boy, and for the boy himself a more subjectivized understanding of the Law. It is as if the symbolic prohibition of murder that drives the Law of the word were only able to be effectively introjected by the subject as its own Law from the moment of its transmission, made possible by the paternal act of renouncing the enjoyment of revenge, so by his liberating submission to the Law of castration.[16]

These examples demonstrate how, in order for the Law of the word to be transmitted from one generation to another, the father – a parent – must apply it first and foremost to himself, he must experience the loss of his own enjoyment. In this sense a father never identifies with the Law, because it is his respect for the Law of the word that makes him a father. Therefore, the Law of castration that he is held to facilitate is not punishment, penance or atonement. The Law of castration is above all that which excludes any possible *enjoyment of the Law*. The father is the symbol of the Law, but only insofar as he is a possibility of its representation who does not enjoy it. His word is the symbol of a Law that humanizes life by separating it from the animal. The father acts as the bringer of the Law that prohibits incestuous enjoyment and, at the same time, as he who offers in inheritance the sense of the Law not as punishment but as a possibility for freedom, as the foundation of desire. The father must facilitate not so much the anonymous universal of the Law in itself, but its more radical humanization. What does it mean then to transmit the Law as a humanized Law? It means transmitting the Law not in opposition to desire, but as its support. Indeed, Lacan states that 'the true function of the father [...] is to unite (and not oppose) a desire to the Law'.[17] The father does not possess the Law, he does not know the ultimate meaning of the world, he cannot make the final judgement on what is just or unjust, but he knows how to demonstrate, through the testimony embodied in his existence, that it is possible, that it is always possible to give *a meaning* to this world, to give a *meaning* to just and unjust. The task of paternal testimony is that of making it possible to give the world meaning. But it is also that of transmitting desire from one generation to the next, of transmitting the meaning of the future. Everything has not already happened, everything has not already been seen, everything is not already known. To inherit is not just to receive the meaning of the world, but to also receive the possibility of opening new meanings of the world, new worlds of meaning. For this reason, as we will see more clearly later on, inheritance is not a turning towards the past but a 'repetition', as Kierkegaard explained in his own way, a *retreating advance*.[18]

## *We Are a Scream in the Night*

The existence of a new discontent of Civilization, which is eloquently demonstrated by the epidemic spread of new forms of symptoms (drug addiction, panic, depression, pathological dependencies, anorexia, bulimia and so on), suggests a profound crisis in the process of symbolic filiation. Life appears to be uncoupled from meaning. Meaning gives way beneath the insistent blows of deadly enjoyment, as a new (perverse) form of the Law. The unnervingly widespread occurrence of depression, even among the new generations, provides an emblematic illustration of this difficulty in preserving the transmission of desire between generations. Nonetheless, there rests an unassailable truth to which the experience of psychoanalysis offers support on a daily basis: in order for life to be truly alive a transmission of desire from one generation to the next is necessary. Human life is 'human' precisely because it cannot be reduced to the mere satisfaction of needs. Life is human when it is animated by the transcendence of desire as the desire of the Other. It is the exposure and opening to, and the demand for love and meaning made to the Other.

Life as such, as an event of nature, as animal life, grips on to life. Life wants to live. Life is the will for life, the will for the repetition of oneself. There is no difference from this point of view when you observe a child or a cat being suckled by their own mother. Life is a hunger for life, driven on by survival, one's urge for self-affirmation. Life wants life. What needs to happen for life to be humanized? For Lacan, the primary location of the humanization of life is in the *scream*. We have all been screams lost in the night. But what is a scream? In the human, it expresses *the demand for life to enter into the order of meaning, it expresses life as an appeal to the Other*. The scream searches in the solitude of the night for a response from the Other. In this sense, even before learning to pray, and even more so in a time in which praying is no longer like breathing, *we are a prayer to the Other*.[19] Life can only enter into the order of meaning if the scream is caught by the Other, by its presence, and is heard. Only if the Other responds to our prayer. Only if this presence translates it into an appeal. This is the primary event in which life is humanized: when the scream is translated into a radical form of demand, when the scream becomes a demand for love, a demand not for something, not for an object, but for the sign of the desire of the Other, for the demand of the present presence of the Other. It is the help offered by the Other that extracts life from its absolute abandonment, from the vulnerability that accompanies its arrival in the world.[20] By responding to the scream, the Other extracts life from its animal depths and saves it from the horror of the night, assigning it a particular place in its desire, in the desire of the Other. This obviously does not mean cancelling out the fact that we are, in the most profound depths of our existence, screams lost in the night, that the translation of the scream into a demand for love cannot help but leave a real remainder that is impossible to translate. This is demonstrated by all of those painful experiences of abandonment and loss we have had in our lives that cause these dark depths to rise up again, this chaotic, anxiety-ridden sensation of being in the most absolute abandonment, of being nothing more than a scream lost in the night. This is what happens in an enigmatic, heart-rending scene recounted by Lacan, in which a child (who? One of his patients? A relation? His son?), faced with the indifference of the Other, literally becomes a dead weight, a life without life, leaving his little body to dangle incapable of reciprocating an embrace he has never received:

I, too, have seen with my own eyes, opened by maternal divi-
nation, the child traumatised by the fact that I was going away
despite the appeal, precociously adumbrated in his voice, and
henceforth more renewed for months at a time – long after,
having picked up this child – I have seen it let his head fall on
my shoulder, and drop off to sleep, sleep alone being capable of
giving him access to the living signifier that I had become since
the date of the trauma.[21]

To fall asleep, switch off, let itself fall like a dead weight: these are the body's responses when faced with traumatic abandonment by the Other. It also occurs in adults. It is no coincidence that the regression to the senseless root of life is central to the treatment of depression when the subject is experiencing an unbearable absence of meaning in their own life, when they are falling like a dead weight into the void of the night. Without the response of the Other, life falls into discomfort. For this reason the screams of the children afflicted with polio who desperately invoke 'their families' through their tears, 'searching in vain for a face they knew', as described by Philip Roth in *Nemesis*, appear like pieces of the real that no symbolic order, not even that of God, can reabsorb. They are a protrusion of life into non-sense, compared to which any religious interpretation comes across as childish hubris. It is the scandal addressed by the book of Job: the pain of existence challenges the order of meaning, demonstrating its structural inconsistency. Faced with this scandal, Bucky, the protagonist of Roth's book, does not give in. He demands that the tragedy of the polio epidemic that has ravaged his city, in which he is implicated – in an ironic splitting – as both the first defender of the poor victims and the healthy carrier of the illness, also be one of guilt. It is this that the narrative voice cannot tolerate:

That the polio epidemic among the children of the Weequahic section and the children of Camp Indian Hill was a tragedy, he could not accept. He has to convert tragedy into guilt. He has to find a necessity for what happens. There is an epidemic and he needs a reason for it. He needs to ask why. Why? Why? That it is pointless, contingent , preposterous and tragic will not satisfy him. Instead he looks desperately for a deeper cause, this martyr, this maniac of the why, and finds the why either in God or in himself or, mystically, mysteriously, in their dreadful joining together as the sole destroyer.[22]

This is the same tragedy faced by Father Paneloux, the pastor of the town invaded by the plague in the famous novel by Albert Camus.[23] His two sermons follow different lines of reasoning. In the first, the event of the plague is understood to be motivated by God's intention to punish, and therefore given a meaning. Humankind deserves the misfortune it finds. The trauma of the plague forces him to reflect upon his own sins. The impetuous domination of the illness and death, particularly that of innocents, of children, pushes Father Paneloux to an absolute change in register. In his second sermon, by which time the plague has ravaged the entire city, and having 'watched a child's agony minute by minute', the emphasis is no longer on the redeeming intentions of God, but on his castration, the castration of God, on the nonsensical and entirely absurd nature of the tragedy of the plague that no symbolic system will ever be able to absorb into the order of meaning. The suffering of the innocent remains an impenetrable scandal that resists any attempts to decipher it. Faced with this indecipherability, it is no longer possible to invoke God's divine plan. Father Paneloux must instead acknowledge the scandal of the senselessness of evil by attempting nevertheless to 'be the one who stays!', like those few heroic monks who remained at the Mercy Monastery as it was devastated by the great plague of Marseilles. [24]

## *Escape from Freedom*

In his film *Salò*, Pasolini describes hell on earth. But what, as Lucretius would ask, really is hell on earth? Hell on earth is not the discontent of Civilization discussed by Freud and other psychoanalysts. This discontent is inevitable because it is the effect of the antagonism between the headless insistence of drives that want to be immediately satisfied and the programme of Civilization that imposes on it the delay of that same satisfaction. This is not how hell is brought to earth. Freud believed the discontent of Civilization was not hell, but something that defines the human condition itself. Civilization demands a domestication, a civilization of the drives. It imposes upon humankind, to use a phrase borrowed from Freud, a 'renunciation of drives' in exchange for it to be recognised as human. It entails a sacrifice of enjoyment as the condition for being included in the community of speakers and mortals. The Law of the word exiles the drives from the body. One cannot enjoy the closest, consecutive object, the forbidden object. One cannot enjoy the maternal Thing. A longer path must be taken, familiar objects must be abandoned. There must be a detachment from the maternal body and a venturing out into the world.

So when does hell on earth occur? The twentieth century, more than any other, knew hell during the terrifying season of totalitarianism that devastated the West. Fascism, Nazism, Stalinism, all drove the delirious, titanic fantasy of a crazed and bloodthirsty Father. What was its harsh lesson? That humankind tends to refuse its own freedom, that it experiences its freedom as a burden that provokes anxiety. The psychology of the totalitarian masses dramatically demonstrates how self-sacrifice, the sacrifice of one's own freedom, or, as Erich Fromm would say, the *escape from freedom*,[25] drives the fanatical adhesion to the Cause (of History, of Race, of Nature). It demonstrates the human race's herd-like tendency to liberate themselves from their own freedom in order to take refuge in the great social body of the undivided mass, in a mass identification (which Wilfred Bion would call 'mindless').[26] The totalitarian utopias of the twentieth century were all built upon the rejection of the Law of the word, proclaiming the Lucretian folly of 'everyone wanting everything'. The twentieth century was a century of mass madness. Nietzsche had demonstrated how human beings were not yet ready for freedom. There is a tendency in humans to refuse freedom, to passively settle down, to take refuge in the herd, to enjoy their own sacrifice. The masses have renounced their freedom to serve the dark God of the Cause. Nietzsche had warned us, albeit in his own way. The experience of freedom is a vertiginous one, it is profound and provokes anxiety. Are human beings truly capable of being free? Are human beings capable of living in the time of the 'death of God', the time of the absence of any guarantee and the lack of foundations? Are we capable of undertaking the duty imposed on us by our own freedom? Freedom always brings with it a quota of anxiety because it exposes us to the character, always contingent and deprived of all guarantees, of our choice and our actions. Mass madness meant looking for a safe refuge in the body of Ideology from the unbearable anxiety of freedom.

The madness of the twentieth century was, as Hannah Arendt demonstrated so well, the 'madness of ideology'.[27] Without doubt, human beings are human because they live on Ideals and not bread alone, but they are also human because, by living for those Ideals, they can reach the point where they kill, destroy and tear each other to pieces. They can be entirely possessed by the Ideal. Was this not the human insanity, the collective hypnosis that the twentieth century so tragically represented? Hell took the paranoid form of the destruction of the enemy, preferring guilty ignorance and rejecting the truth that reveals how the real enemy lies within themselves; *the impure is in the human being*. It does not enter into the human, but comes from it. This is a subversive point in the teachings of Jesus when it comes to the Jewish tradition that understood purification as exterior rituals such as the washing of hands. This tradition is radically shaken up by Jesus' declaration that 'nothing that enters a person from the outside can defile them' because only 'What comes out of a person is what defiles them.' To those who reprimand his disciples for not respecting the tradition that insists upon the washing of hands and dishes before eating, paranoiacally identifying the impure as a bacterium that is external to the human, an externalized enemy, Jesus asserts the principle that only 'What comes out of a person is what defiles them. For it is from within, out of a person's heart, that evil thoughts come – sexual immorality, theft, murder, adultery, greed, malice, deceit, lewdness, envy, slander, arrogance and folly. All these evils come from inside and defile a person.'[28] We find the same idea in Freud: the barbarian is not other to the subject, but is the being of the drive that I myself am. It serves no purpose, therefore, to destroy the enemy as if it were a bacterium. No hygiene measures are necessary, no hygienic rituals of purification or medical curtains. Evil never comes solely from outside; the most ineradicable evil lives in our very being.

### The Fantasy of Freedom as a Hypermodern Fantasy

Our time seems to cloak the thorny condition of defence-lessness and dereliction that is part of our existence in a false euphoria. Our time sponsors the fetishistic dimension of the Ego as the new idol, which masks (as occurs with the very function of the fetish) the primordial anxiety linked to our condition of defencelessness. The celebration of the Ego, of its autonomy, of its deliberative power and its self-consistency is a cipher symptomatic of our time. This cult of the Ego is, for Lacan, 'the greatest madness'.[29] The hypermodern fantasy of freedom as the spreading out of the Ego is the fundamental manifestation of this madness. To what freedom does it refer? A freedom released from any responsibility. This brings with it the cancellation of one's own provenance, of one's own roots, of the symbolic debt to the Other. *The fantasy of freedom refuses descendence, the very experience of filiation, along with the experience of the limit, it refuses our own existence as children.* The affirmation of the Ego takes place in opposition to the existence of the Other, against the transcendence of the language that imposes the need on the human to subjugate themselves

37

to the Law of the word. Our time refuses this subordination, proclaiming deliriously the human ability to 'go it alone', the rejection of their condition as a child, or, as Lacan would have it, a 'servant' even, of language. Becoming one's own parent is a madness equal to insisting on the Ego as the master of its own house. The freedom derived from this coincides with a fantasy of omnipotence that forestalls the finite nature of existence. This freedom does not come from castration, from finitude (the great theme not just of psychoanalysis but of all philosophical existentialism), but expresses the madness of the Ego as a madness of appropriation of one's own foundations. It is, therefore, freedom that refuses the responsibility that characterizes the unique movement of inheritance. We must not forget that, as Massimo Cacciari correctly reminds us, the term 'heir' comes from the Latin *heres*, which has the same root as the Greek word *cheros*, meaning deserted, bare, lacking. This means that there is no difference between the heir and the orphan, because the person who can truly inherit is 'only whoever discovers themselves to be *orbus, orphanos*'.[30] Every authentic movement of inheritance supposes the incision, the separation, the trauma of the father's abandonment; the experience of loss, of being an orphan. This is the profound tension that characterizes the movement of inheritance, as we will see with the figure of Telemachus. A faithfulness that is passive or soulless does not allow for the subjectivization of our past. Inheritance is not the search for reassurance about our identity. Rather it implies a jump forward, a rip, a dangerous reclamation. Our time refuses the uprooted condition of the heir-orphan in favour of the freedom that would like its foundations to come only from within itself. This is a hallucinatory dimension of freedom. The *homo felix* of the hypermodern manic flight of ideas reduces the tragic undertaking of 'faithfulness to the earth', as discussed by Nietzsche, to a song from a barrel organ: freedom shrugs off all responsibility in order to insist on the assertion of narcissistic enjoyment as enjoyment of the One without the Other. It is in no way a frivolous extension of the immanentism that inhabits the will of Nietzschean power.[31] In Nietzsche, freedom does not ever justify free will but, on the contrary, touches the summit of responsibility: how to live in a world without God? How can human beings give meaning to a world that has been deserted by God? How will they be able to be 'human' in a different way from that version of human that gives the responsibility of freedom to the Idols of metaphysics? Within these questions we must gather all the ethical meaning of Nietzsche's meditations and his appeal for human beings to be truly capable of freedom. Conversely, the *homo felix* – the hypermodern, hyper-hedonistic human – would prefer to dismiss the problem of responsibility as an antiquated one. Freedom offers itself as simply and radically thoughtless. What counts is doing what you want without taking on the consequences of your own actions. Hypermodern freedom separates the act from responsibility. Its roots do not lie in Nietzsche's reflection, which does nothing more than interrogate the possibility of humankind taking upon themselves the limitless weight of responsibility that freedom brings, but in the affirmation of the capitalist discourse which promises salvation through the worship of objects. This is why *the uncoupling of freedom and responsibility* lies at the heart of the hypermodern fantasy of freedom. By severing this tie that binds freedom to responsibility (a bond that stretches from Nietzsche to Heidegger and Sartre), the *homo felix* experiences a degraded freedom that is pure whim. Whim is, in fact, a form of freedom separated from the ethical meaning of responsibility. The irresponsibility of whim lies in its dissolving of the nexus between the act (first and foremost, the act of the word) and its consequences.

## Mass Freedom

Nowadays, hell no longer unleashes the mad flame of ideology. We are facing a new, 'soft' version of totalitarianism. The Freudian discontent of Civilization hails from the experience of renunciation and forces the human to subjugate their lives to the Law of the word. It is not a curse, as we have seen, but the very condition for the humanization of life. The best thing that can happen to us is to be governed, subjected to and subjectivized by the Law of the word. The twentieth century, however, overturned this Law. The dream of every totalitarianism is to find the purity of an Origin (Race, Nature, History) that precedes the Law of the word. The hypermodern version of this has instead renounced any thought of Origin. This new hell originates in a profound distortion of the Freudian discontent of Civilization. Whilst that discontent was generated by the conflict between the programme of the drive and that of Civilization (the act of being civilized brought with it the death of the animal and the sacrifice of drives for humans), today's version seems to be generated by a perverse cult of an enjoyment that is immediate, limitless, absolute, without barriers: an enjoyment without a Cause, an enjoyment that does not enjoy sacrifice but only its own growth and infinite enhancement. This enjoyment, which the machine of the capitalist discourse places widely at our disposal, is no longer one that is limited by the Law of castration, but becomes a new form of Law. The only possible form of Law. The only Law that counts is the Law of enjoyment, an enjoyment that takes on the form of a paradoxical duty, in which, as Lucretius announced, 'everyone wants everything'. Enjoyment is not that which transgresses the Law but the hypermodern version of the Law. From it comes the hyper-hedonistic discontent of Civilization that has been at the heart of much of my work.[32]

What untruth about human beings comes from this new configuration of the discontent of Civilization? Why does this hell imply a new dehumanization of humankind different from the one that dominated during the tragedies of the twentieth century? The fundamental lie, as I have already pointed out, has to do with the notion of freedom. The free person is a person reduced to a pure drive to enjoy, a machine for enjoyment that does not fulfil in any way the promise of liberation seemingly fuelled by that very machine. This new representation of humans is an alternative to the ideological being of the twentieth century because what moves it is not a passion for great ideals, but the compulsive urge for deadly enjoyment. The *homo felix*'s conception of life appears pragmatic and hedonistic. But, as we are taught by psychoanalytic practice, when drive is uncoupled from desire it can only become a death drive. The hypermodern human wants to fully satisfy that urge to enjoy beyond desire. Its question is a radical one: what can give sense to this life if not desperate enjoyment to the point of death? If not the eternal repetition of enjoyment? Is this not the super-egoic imperative of our time? Is this not its fundamental perversion? To enjoy absolutely and beyond the Law of the word! If all ideals are defaced, as Pasolini demonstrates in *Salò*, if they have lost all consistency, all that is left is the human being as a machine for pure enjoyment. It is the cynical, narcissistic trait of our time. Each person claims his or her own right to happiness, as the right to enjoy without intrusion of any kind by the Other. This is a new ideology, an ideology that emerges from the abandonment of all ideology. It agitates for the liberation of desire, radically dissociating the renunciation of drives from meaning. For Freud, this is an effect of the humanization of life produced by the programme of Civilization. This new version of the human being is founded on the deterioration of the experience of desire. What is desire destined to become beyond the Law of the word? It becomes a greedy urge to enjoy one's own life until death. It is reduced to the repetitive and never-satisfied movement of the filling-up of the human being, who is a 'perforated vessel', according to the famous image used by Lucretius.[33] But this filling-up is impossible because the nature of the drive that runs through it is insatiable. *The Blind Leading the Blind*, also known as *The Parable of the Blind*, by the Flemish artist Bruegel,[34] depicting a procession of blind men clinging on to a blind guide, provides an unrivalled portrait of this understanding of desire. A lost procession, moving towards the abyss. Hypermodern desire seems to inhabit the myth of self-expansion, self-aggrandizement, of one's own strengthening, but, in reality, it generates only an infinite procession of objects that fail to satisfy. No object can, in fact, fill that 'perforated vessel' of which the human is made. The saving, medicinal, analgesic power of each object is the second greatest lie of our time. It is as if the new object, the newest object will lead us to salvation. And yet, the vessel remains full of holes. Insatiable desire consumes all objects and those who consume them. There is no freedom here, just coercion, serfdom, pathological dependency. Insatiable desire only generates enslavement. Not mass freedom, as promised by the capitalist discourse, but only anonymous oppression. The paradox that commands hypermodern freedom is that it is not free. The New becomes an imperative of the Super-Ego, revealing itself to be the flip-side of the Same. That which is infinitely repeated is actually the same dissatisfaction. The hypermodern hell consists of the reduction of freedom to the arbitrary purity of whim. It is the ongoing party of the night of the Proci, with no respect for the Law of the word. Desire is transformed into compulsive enjoyment. The discontent of Civilization no longer takes on the face of sacrifice and the renunciation of drives, but the dazed face of the bulimic, the drug addict, the alcoholic, of the panic-stricken, of apathetic and carefree youth. Drive is detached from desire and no longer obeys the Law of the word in any way: it is the pure will to want everything.

And yet desire does not only have this tyrannical and dissatisfied face of insatiable desire. It is also that which resists the dominance of deadly enjoyment. What can save life from this new form of enslavement? Desire as vocation, as openness, a strength that transcends the immediacy of consumption. It is desire that does not believe in the saving power of the object and its compulsive nature. It is desire that does not blindly follow the mirage of the New, but that extracts the New of faithfulness from the same because it knows how to make the same things New. This strength, the power of desire, is not the antithesis of responsibility but a radical and limitless form of responsibility. In the *Odyssey*, Odysseus, father of Telemachus, reveals this in his use of a bow and arrow. It requires strength guided by memory, a knowing strength, enough to reach its own lost part. The string bends, it does not reject the hands of those that know how to recognize it, of those who, in turn, bend to its strength.[35]

## Dying to Work

The Law of the word imposes a detachment from the most familiar objects, subverting the natural order of immediacy and imposing the delay of enjoyment. But this delay, as we have already said, is not in any way a curse. The most successful form of the delay or sublimation of drive is *work*, which Hegel by no means coincidentally defined as an 'appetite held at bay'. Through work a human form is given to the world, an endeavour is made, life is humanized. Work, as Marx had entirely understood, is a profound expression of the programme of Civilization. It is the point at which the strength of the drive produces the form of the world. It is only the alienated estrangement of work that leads to a collapse of meaning, but work in itself, as a human manifestation of the praxis, is a form of human fulfilment. It is not a collapse of meaning, but that which gives meaning to life, as demonstrated by the growing number of suicides during the current period of economic crisis. Hell is being stripped of one's own work, of the possibility of making life human by differentiating it from that of animals. For this reason, the word 'work' is at the centre of the discourse of the subject at this time of great uncertainty. Patients do not talk only of their enslavement, their symptoms, but also of work as an opportunity for redemption. Indeed, in work there is not just exploitation, the brutality of Capital, subjugation of life, as an ideologically impoverished application of Marxism would have us believe. Work in itself, as Marx himself demonstrated, does not coincide at all with alienation. The demand of youth has never been the *demand for work* to the extent it is now. Is Telemachus' gaze, open towards the sea, not a gaze that waits for work as an opportunity to give meaning to his own presence in the world?

One of the consequences of the Japanese economic crisis at the end of the 1990s was a significant rise in the number of suicides. The victims were predominantly men over the age of fifty who found themselves marginalized by industrial restructuring programmes. They often chose to throw themselves under trains as they arrived in the station. The widespread nature of this phenomenon led a Tokyo-based train company to install so-called 'anti-suicide mirrors'. Japanese psychologists thought that returning an image of themselves to the subject would have a dissuasive effect: seeing my image as a man in the mirror should curb my suicidal urge. An injection of narcissism should work to offset the depressive sentiment that would lead to the grave. A naïve thought. The image of ourselves is not the image reflected in the mirror, but that reflected by society, by the people we love and respect, the people who recognize our value. The mirror that counts is the mirror that restores to us our dignity as human beings. It is for this reason, according to Winnicott, who draws on Lacan, that the real mirror is the face of the mother. Those who decide to commit suicide are people who have lost their own image, who have met with a smashed mirror, who cannot recognize themselves in anything. They have been stripped of their own image because they have lost the possibility of work, as the possibility that assigns dignity and value to life, humanizing it, and fulfilling it socially.

Man shall not live on bread alone, goes the famous Evangelical maxim. Psychoanalysts are by no means the only people to see its truth borne out on a daily basis: human life is not just fulfilled through the meeting of natural and instinctive basic needs. Life is only humanized through the acquisition of a symbolic dignity that renders it unique and irreplaceable. Life is humanized through its recognition by its own family and the society to which it belongs as a human life. Faced with the tragic rash of suicides caused by loss of work, professional failure, or anxiety about not being able to bear the continuous increase in debt and the seismic wave of the economic crisis we are experiencing, we are reminded of the potency of this Evangelical maxim. Not that bread is not important. Who could possibly deny this, particularly in times of crisis when the very survival of individuals and their families is endangered? And yet the tragedy of suicide is truly human (and solely human) because it is not *bread alone* that is at stake. The lack of bread can be disheartening, and generate indignation, struggle, legitimate demands for social justice, desperation, frustration. But it is not the lack of bread in itself that can lead to a decision to leave the world. Marx was right to refuse to consider work as a mere means of sustenance. He believed that humans would find in work not only the means to earn their daily bread, but also and most importantly, the opportunity to give their lives meaning, to make their life different from that of an animal, to render it human. It is work that gives shape to the world, that transforms its very fabric, that leads to endeavour, construction, planning; that knows how to generate the future. This is what led Marx to attribute a fundamental and unique dignity to human work.[36] This is why work is not primarily a source of alienation, but the opportunity for fulfilment in life. It does not steal our life but constitutes it as human. And yet we have known times in which work in itself (and not its capitalist expropriation as per Marx's classic thesis) is culturally rejected as a source of alienation and brutalization of life. I am obviously referring here to work and not its material conditions, which can animalize life, insult it, exploiting it brutally. The thesis of work being set against life rather than being a condition of its humanization is the theme of a certain naïve libertarianism that conditioned the 1968 movement and that has reached us through the 1970s. Today, this culture ends up (as Lacan had foretold) fatally colluding with the hyper-hedonism that feeds the capitalist discourse: work is nothing more than a limit, a burden, an affliction, an evil. It is better to make money in other, quicker and less laborious ways. Better to take a shortcut, the path in thrall to an economic house of cards that is financial and speculative, rather than taking the long way round, filled with obstacles such as work. The ideology of the liberation of desire leads straight to the blind refusal of work as a form of brutalization of human life. But what would happen to an economy without work? How could it keep itself going, how could it generate wealth? This is the great illusion of the financial economy that has pushed the West towards the abyss of crisis.[37]

In *Cosa resta del padre?* [*What Remains of the Father?*] I had emphasized a fatal error present in the legitimate objection raised by the 1968 student movement to the disciplinary and authoritarian versions of the Law, embodied by the father-as-master. Truly emancipating oneself from the father does not mean rejecting his very existence. In order to do without the father, as Lacan says, you have to know how to make him serve you. The refusal of the father chains you to him forever; hate does not liberate but binds for eternity, creating only monsters, obstructing the deployment of life. The rhetoric, deliriously sponsored by our times, that one can become their own parent fails to recognize that no human life can be constituted by itself. By rejecting paternity one rejects also the symbolic debt that makes filiation possible from one generation to the next. Freedom is uncoupled from responsibility and becomes pure whim, a triumph of perversion. Things are no different when it comes to work. The ideological refusal of work as a location of the mortification of life today contrasts very clearly with the desperate demand for our right to it, for the possibility for it to exist and for it to be provided. People are killing themselves, not to free themselves from work but to reclaim (albeit in a destructive way) their dignity as human beings, to be able to fulfil their own human essence *through work*, as the young Marx would say. Inheritance as a movement of subjectivization passes through the possibility of work. Is this not perhaps one of the reasons that drove Odysseus, Telemachus' father, on against the wasteful arrogance of the Proci? Against them losing themselves in an enjoyment without satisfaction? Against their refusal of work?

2

# The Confusion Between Generations

## *The Parents' Task*

Freud said that the parents' task is an impossible one. Just, he added, like governing or psychoanalysing. This means that the parent's job cannot be modelled on an ideal, because the ideal does not exist. Every parent is called to educate their children with their own inadequacy as the only starting point, exposing themselves to the risk of error and failure. For this reason, the best parents are those who offer themselves to their children not as models, but as fully aware of the impossible nature of their task. This is good news that should relieve the anxiety of those who find themselves in this position. Psychoanalytic treatment confirms this truth mercilessly. The worst parents – those who do their children most damage – are not just those who abandon their responsibilities, avoiding the educational task that is theirs to carry out, but also those who misrecognize their own inadequacy, those who rather than submit themselves to the Law of the word (as they ask their children to do) presumptuously believe they embody it themselves. They are educational parents, who use their knowledge as though it were a power and vice versa. They are those who insist they are explaining the meaning of life because they believe they are *proprietors* of their children's lives. They are also those who, rather than welcoming the Law of the word and becoming its custodians, always presume to have the right to the final word on all things. This is the greatest aberration afflicting the figure of the parent-as-educator, and in a privileged way, that of the father who in this case is no longer (as he should be) the one who knows how to give the word, how to carry the word, but he who considers it his exclusive right to impose it, as if it were an absolute power.

This depiction of the parent-as-educator is not, however, the only way of nullifying the impossibility presented by the impossible task of being a parent. At the moment, it is not so much the parent-as-educator that dominates but its mirror image: the figure of the *parent-as-child*. These are parents who abdicate their own role, not because they abandon their children or because they present themselves as exemplary educators, but because they are too close, too similar to their children. The worst are no longer those who see themselves as entrusted with an educational task experienced as a redemptive mission (parents as professional educators), but those who symmetrically assimilate the youth of their children. The child-as-Narcissus is reflected in the parent-as-child, and vice versa. The symbolic difference between generations leaves space for their fundamental confusion. To borrow a phrase from Pasolini, this is a recent 'anthropological mutation': the evaporation of adults, who have vanished in the face of their educational responsibilities.

The impossible task of parents is today charged with new anxieties. To say that our time is that of the symbolic crisis in the function of parental authority is blindingly obvious. This does not just mean that fathers and parents are in a state of crisis, but that the Law of the word seems to have lost its symbolic foundations. If ours is a time of the 'evaporation of the father', it is because it is a time of the 'evaporation of the Law of the word' as that which safeguards the possibility for humans to live together. The symptoms of this evaporation are clear for all to see and they not only besiege the psycho-analyst's office (anxiety-ridden parents, lost children, families in a state of chaos) but run through the entire social body: a difficulty in instilling respect for institutions, the collapse of public morality, the eclipsing of the educational discourse, the breakdown in a sense of shared life, an inability to build creative social ties, the triumph of a deadly enjoyment uncoupled from desire, and so on. At the forefront is not so much a cultural weakening of the laws written in the legal Codes and in the books of Law, but of the very meaning of the Law of the word that, as psychoanalysis teaches and as we have seen, has as its fundamental characteristic the sustaining of human life as marked by a lack, by a sense of the limit, by an impossibility of self-sufficiency.

This cultural weakening of the Law of the word does not just generate bewilderment, but the symptom of a compulsive invocation of the written laws, in the form of the appeal reiterated to the judges, the courts and the norms established by the Code. It is another characteristic of our time: *the Law is continually invoked when there is a fault in the transmission of the symbolic meaning of the Law*. The evanescence of the symbolic

Law of the word increases unsustainable recourse to the Law. Psychoanalytic practice defines the tendency to continually invoke the intervention of the Law of the Code as a supplement to the subject's lacking inscription in the Law of the word, as 'querulomania'.[1] This describes a real and persecutory use of the Law that, in reality, attempts to cover the void left by the foreclosure of the symbolic Law of the word. But the Law does not threaten punishment, it is not a form of vendetta, it bears no grudge. Even Telemachus insists on invoking it, as we see in the opening of the 'Telemachy' when, following the goddess' advice, he calls the people's assembly to place the arrogance of the Proci before the Law of the word, but his invocation is in no way querulomaniacal.[2] In querulomania, which is a 'legalistic' declension of paranoia, *recourse to the Law of Right takes place in opposition to the Law of the word*. It refers only to an aggressive use of the Law, whilst Telemachus awaits the Law of the word to clear away the deadly aggression that has sprung from the failure of respect for the symbolic difference between generations. Odysseus returns to kill the sons that do not respect the Law of the word, which is the *Law of hospitality*. In the following pages I will try to demonstrate how the Telemachus complex configures itself as a possible key to understanding the hypermodern discontent of youth. Unlike the querulomaniac, who would like the Law to be *ad personam*, the expectation held by Odysseus' son is that there be a possibility for justice in the city, in the *polis*; he invokes the Law not to oppress life but to liberate it.

The current querulomaniacal development of the appeal to juridical Law compensates for parents' difficulty in fostering respect for the Law of the word in this time of confusion between generations. The compulsive invocation of the Law of Codes seems to speak to the difficulty adults encounter in exercising the symbolic function of the Law. *The inactivity of the symbolic Other tends to call upon the Other of the court in a hyperactive way.* This is what happens in modern families. There are courts that hear cases of children mistreated by adults and of those that aid adults in their conjugal diatribes. The institution of family mediation seems to have become indispensable in the resolution of conflicts that risk degenerating.[3] A situation that is even more paradoxical if one considers that it is often the children that impose and act as the Law within a family. It is they who, rather than submitting to the rules, dictate them. We have a great anthropological mutation: it is no longer the child that must adapt to the symbolic norms that regulate the life of a family, but the families that adapt to the Law established at the whim of their children.[4] The call for a judge to intercede is a sign of this profound alteration in symbolic roles. It is a hypermodern paradox: the parents, who have increasing difficulty in transmitting the meaning of the Law of the word to their children, appeal to the Law of the judge so that they may restore the parents' ownership over the children!

Violence, abuse and disorder have always characterized human relationships, including those within families. Conflict is a part of life. The Law of the word does not eliminate the harsh nature of human relationships, but makes possible their inclusion in a discourse. Why then has the intervention of a third party capable of semaphorically regulating the disorder in the most intimate of emotional relationships become increasingly necessary? It is with growing frequency that family problems end up before a judge or require mediation from a Third. At a time in which the Third no longer seems to exist, at a time in which everything appears equal to everything else, in which the difference between generations seems to have been swallowed up by a confusing identification of parents with children, the Third tends to be called upon every single time an obstacle is encountered in the pursuit of one's own interests, or those of one's child. Parents have no problem breaking the generational pact with teachers if it means their child, unfairly judged, does not have to repeat a year, and every intervention by a Third is viewed with suspicion and diffidence, as if it were an abuse of power.[5] 'Why don't they separate if all they do is argue?', a very young patient asked himself. When he dared ask his parents this question, they replied in unison: 'And what would you do without us?', insinuating that they were sacrificing themselves for his own good. The response: 'Would I have to die for you two to finally leave one another?' The ironclad logic of this little boy leaves no way out for his parents, who are rightly tormented by the assumption of their educational responsibilities. We know that being a parent can never be conflated with the sometimes stormy fate of the couple. We know how children can be swept up in the terrible tide of reciprocal recriminations between spouses. It is then, for example, that the urgent intervention of a Third is called upon. But should the judge intervene on behalf of the children or the adults? Does their increasingly commonplace invocation not perhaps suggest a *generalized minorization of adults*, in the sense that it proves how the strength to take on the decision-making responsibility that comes with every educational act seems to have failed them? Here, that responsibility is being delegated to the judge. But why must the Third necessarily be embodied by a judge if the Law of the word does not identify with that of the Codes? Should the Third not appear instead as the recognition of the symbolic meaning of the Law of the word, one that insists parents care for their children beyond their own personal interests? The symbolic meaning of the Law today is either discredited or entirely confused with the material existence of the Codes. Thus widespread querulomania reveals, in its continual recourse to the Law of Right, a defect in the subjectivization of the Law of the word that invests the adult world. To restore value to the symbolic character of the Law would imply parents know how to renounce the narcissistic expectations of their children. The educational act carries with it the destiny of separation that accompanies the parents' relationship with their children. Knowing how to lose one's own children is the greatest gift a parent can give, and it begins at the point at which they take on the responsibility of representing the Law of the word. To be parents, as the scandalous biblical tale of the sacrifice of Isaac reminds us, implies above all else the radical renunciation of the ownership of one's children, the knowing how to 'give [them] up to the wilderness'.[6]

## *The Law and the laws*

Community life is made possible by the symbolic mediation imposed by the Law of the word. Human life is fulfilled through the language that imposes on it a continual and demanding exercise in translation: I become what I am only by passing through the mediation of the Other (be it family, institutions, society, culture, work, and so on). Today, many psychoanalysts can see how this institutional mediation that is necessary for life is in crisis.[7] All institutions are finding themselves in difficulty when it comes to safeguarding their role as the Third. Working in the collective interest is seen as an abuse of power against the freedom of the individual. A strong wind blows in the opposite direction to the symbolic function of institutions. There are many examples of this wind and they affect our daily life. When faced with failing a year, parents tend to side with their children rather than the teachers. They change school or take their cause to the judges at the local administrative court. The assumption of an educational position arouses suspicion that power is being applied in an arbitrary fashion. The Internet offers the possibility for those who believe themselves to be authors to publish their own book online, without having to face the scrutiny of an editor. Friendships no longer pass through the indispensable mediation of the encounter, but are cultivated anonymously on social networks. When faced with the necessarily exasperating dimension of political conflict, violence, insult and calculated defamation of the adversary are the preferred option. Even the symptoms that afflict people's lives have changed. Whilst a decade ago they seemed to be centred on trials of love and the inalienable importance of social ties, today it is not the breaking of a bond that causes suffering, but the existence of a bond that is refused as a source of discontent. This leads to the formation of new mono-symptomatic groups of anorexics, depressives, those suffering from panic attacks, drug addicts, each gathered around their own fetishistic sign.[8] What is perhaps the most disturbing example affects the young. Millions of young people live in the so-called civilized world as voluntary prisoners, closed in their rooms. They have severed all ties with the world; they have withdrawn from life, abandoned school and work. This anonymous multitude prefers its autistic withdrawal, the narcissistic turning in on oneself, to the difficulties of the trans-lation imposed by the Law of the word. It is a sign of our times. The Third increasingly appears as an intruder. And yet there is no human life that is not constituted through the symbolic mediation of the Other. The anxiety-ridden cry of a child in the night calls us to respond, to be present; it summons us in our limitless responsibility to embrace their life. The myth of being self-made, of self-generation, like that of carrying out justice on our own, remains, at least as far as psychoanalysis is concerned, a fascist myth. No one is master of their own origins, just as no one can be the saviour of the world. No human community can exist without institutional mediation, without symbolic media-tion, without the patient work of translation.

This decline of symbolic mediation does not just mean that we have lost the guiding light of the great Ideals of modernity and are scurrying about without a compass, outside the clear lines set down by the world's great ideological narratives (Catholicism, Socialism, Communism, etc.) and their disciplinary institutions (Church, State, Army). This decline demonstrates, as Pasolini would say, that there has been a real 'anthropological mutation' of life. Our time is one in which individualism asserts itself in its most cynical and narcissistic guise, regarding the institutional dimension of symbolic mediation with radical suspicion: all institutions that should guarantee community life serve no purpose. At best, they are dead weights, archaic burdens that hold back the individual's will for affirmation, and at worst, places of squandering and obscene corruption. How has this happened? Is it not, as Lacan declared, the task of institutions to put the brakes on individual enjoyment, rendering the social pact, a shared life, possible?

The violence of this economic crisis has produced a rightful distrust of everything that acts in the name of public life, towards everything that escapes direct control by the citizen. Institutions have been incapable of warning, preventing, governing. Politics provides a perfect example. The location that should be able to determine the public integration of individual difference under the sign of the good of the *polis* — the most eminent location of the exercise of symbolic translation — has revealed itself to have been corrupted by the most foolish assertions of individual interests. The political human, freed from the weight of ideology, has been reduced to a scoundrel who steals only for themselves.[9] Lacan's response to the criticism levelled by the students in 1968, who reprimanded him for not authorizing the revolt against the institutions, was that there is no 'outside' of the mediation imposed by language. The destiny of talking-beings is, in fact, that of translation, of being thrown into, exposed to the language of the Other. In 1968, Lacan disappoints the students' revolutionary fervour, declaring it impossible for a revolt driven by a rupture with the institutional field of language not to fall into the same violence from which it would like to free itself. Revolution always leads back to its point of departure, bringing with it a new master.[10] We have been taught this by history and, in a more modest way, by the practice of psychoanalysis. Anger towards fathers, the wholesale refusal of everything that has been received, the negation of our status as heirs, always risks generating a sterile protest that leads us into the dark tunnel of violence and insult that stops us from telling the difference between gold and mud, that throws the baby out with the bath-water and, last but not least, keeps us forever bound to the father from whom we wanted to free ourselves, revealing once more his monstrous and authoritarian face.

## Adulterations

Parents seem to be lost in the same sea in which their children lose themselves every day. At the forefront we no longer have the generational difference but the *confusion between generations*. It is increasingly difficult to grow up in a world that dreams of eternal youth and rejects the real experience of the impossible. This reduction of subjective responsibility to zero is a cipher of our time. A recent American comedy, *Young Adult* by Jason Reitman, seems (judging solely by the title) to gauge the temperature of this strange fever overtaking the adult world. In this film, death is celebrated as a mirage of regeneration; the adulteration of the adult would consist in its regression to stubborn immaturity, to the (impossible) recovery of time passed, to a refusal to take on that limitless responsibility implied by their role. The plot is both disarming and eloquent: a divorced ex-writer who, without once considering the irreversibility of time, returns to her small town in Minnesota to win back her high school sweetheart, who, in the meantime, is married and has a child.

What is happening? If an adult is someone who tries to accept the consequences of their actions and words (this is a definition of 'adult' that I would like to propose, beyond its dictionary definition) then we cannot help but note a strong decline in their presence in today's society. Think of all those people who, invested with institutional roles, doggedly pursue their own personal interests rather than serving collective ones. Think of those figures of *puer aeternus* who have governed us and have conditioned the collective imaginary, offering themselves as models for a free enjoyment, emancipated from castration and unburdened by the Law of the word. But think also of Captain Schettino,[11] who, in order to flaunt his reckless phallic potency, risks the lives of thousands of people as if he were in a videogame. Or those parents who, rather than supporting one another in their educational roles, promptly desert them, proving themselves ready to defend the inconsistent reasons cited by their children against teachers or at the first sign of difficulty shown by life.

Adults seem to be lost in the same sea as their children, with no generational distinction. They pursue easy friendships on the various social networks, they dress like their children, they play their games, they speak the same language, they have the same ideals. This new portrait of the adult praises the immortal myth of Peter Pan, the myth of perennial youth, the rhetoric of a cult of immaturity that proposes a carefree happiness, freed of all responsibility.[12] It is a cipher of our time: 'My father', a daughter of separated parents, desolately confided in me, 'does nothing but chase my friends and then asks if he can talk to me about it!' In short, is it not the case that the real *bamboccioni*[13] are today's adults rather than their children? In this sense, Schettino's dialogue with Captain Gregorio De Falco has come to constitute a real paradigm: it does not just tell the tale of a dramatic clash between two men in a situation of great tension and danger, but it flags up a *split within the generation of adults*, between those who assume (or attempt to assume) the full weight of their actions, and those who would instead like to keep on playing life as if it were a PlayStation. There are, of course, many examples, but they all converge on one fact: *the solitude of the new generations* (which defines the position of Telemachus awaiting his father's return) hails from the difficulty shown by adults in shouldering the limitless responsibility implied by their educational role.

## *Transgression or an Appeal to the Law?*

There is a moralistic and classically Oedipal model that defines the relationship between desire and the Law. It is the one that couples the Law with its transgression, which sees desire and its structurally perverse and polymorphic urge on one side, and the moral and rigidly repressive authority of the Law on the other. It is a version of the Law that has at its centre an antagonism with desire. I would add that it offers only a phantasmatic and pathological (neurotic) version of the Law. In this model, the Law founds the possibility of transgression insofar as it sets up a boundary, it defines the normative limit that desire tends to transgressively surpass. In this case it is the Law that sins, according to the famous formula by Paul of Tarsus, repeated many times by Lacan. Our time obliges us, however, to update this Oedipal model of the relationship between Law and desire.

A patient in his fifties told me of the thrill that would permeate him when, as a boy, he would slip into the town library and smuggle out books he could not afford to buy. In the compulsive repetition of the act of stealing, it was not the object-book at the forefront, but the subject's relationship with the Law and the 'strange' excitement that accompanied the transgressive act of stealing. This excitement signalled a barrier being crossed, giving rise to a sense of getting round the Law. In this case, the transgression necessarily implied the existence of the Law, its solid presence, because without it, there would be no excitement at all as the very meaning of transgression would have failed.

A young bulimic patient told me of her irresistible tendency to steal from supermarkets. It was a real kleptomaniacal impulse (sometimes accompanied by forms of amnesia that would stop her from remembering what she had stolen) that she could not control. These robberies, like those of the patient in his fifties, do not revolve around the stolen objects, which the subject would abandon indifferently. But in this case, they are not committed in order to repeat the thrill of transgression, of challenging or getting round the Law. These robberies do not revolve around the Law. The illegality of this behaviour corresponds to a reason that turns the Oedipal dynamic of transgression, through which the most desired object is that which is most vehemently prohibited, on its head. It is the object subjected to the symbolic prohibition of the Law of castration. What new lesson can we draw from this young patient's kleptomania? She insists on going beyond the Law, she insists on repeating an act that is outside the Law, but *only so as to be seen, to be recognized, to make the Other of the Law exist*. The act is not repeated in order to defraud the Law, to enjoy the perverse chills of subtracting oneself from its gaze, but, paradoxically, in order to *give the Law a body*. Does anyone see me? Is there a Law that can still help me not to lose myself? Is there another Other capable of stopping me, of bringing into existence a limit on deadly enjoyment? This girl's desperate kleptomania demonstrates how the person who has truly been robbed is the subject. Throughout her life she had never encountered a 'No!' from her parents, too preoccupied with cultivating their own sentimental relationships to deal with her, a 'No!' that was precisely that: symbolic prohibition as a gift of the Law of the word, as a gift that humanizes life. But not even her parents were able to give her a word that truly concerned her, they had never listened to her word. 'I mean nothing to them', she would repeat, sadly monotonous. In her passage to the act of stealing *there is no enjoyment of transgression, but an invocation of the Law, an invocation of the Other of the word*. Why have you forsaken me? Why can you not see me? Why do you not realize I exist?

This young woman is not simply defrauding the Law or enjoying the thrill of her transgression. In a paradoxical way she is doing exactly the opposite: she is trying to be seen, to be noticed by the Law, to *make the Law exist*. Is there a Law, or simply an adult, anywhere at all who can answer me, who can recognize my existence?

This girl's demand is the same as that made by many young people, and is a demand that is insistent and places us with our backs against the wall: do you still exist? Do adults still exist? Is there still someone who knows how to take responsibility for the weight of their own word and their own actions? In this girl's kleptomania we can find the cipher of the contemporary discontent of youth. At its centre is no longer the Oedipal conflict between generations, the conflict between the Law and its transgressive subversion, but the solitude of one generation that feels it has been left to fall, abandoned, that searches for contact with the adult world but cannot find it, that struggles to find any adult against whom to measure their own project for the world. The great current crisis in capitalist economy, and the real risk of our collective material and mental impoverishment, amplifies this fact, making it even more decisive. What kind of world are we leaving for the new generations to inherit? What can we do to return hope to a broken Telemachus? How can we show the young kleptomaniac that a trustworthy Law does exist, one that is capable of seeing and recognizing her existence? Is this not what can save her from solitude and abandonment? Is this not what lies behind Telemachus' hope? The bulimic girl who steals from supermarkets, is her name not the same as Telemachus? Is there no one capable of reading in her transgression the insistence of a symbolic demand for recognition? Is this not what our children are effectively asking us for? If the adult's place remains empty, deserted, repudiated, it will be difficult for the new generations to feel recognized, it will be difficult for them to truly feel like children. Whose children? Belonging to which parent, which adult? To which testimony of life?

To be clear: the adult is not bound to embody any model of perfection, any normative ideal. Rather, as I have already said, among the very worst examples we must also catalogue those that offer themselves to the young generations as ideals. If a parent does not demonstrate their own relationship with the impossible, with their own castration, how will they be able to transmit this meaning to their children? If in their actions an adult misrecognizes the symbolic meaning of the Law of the word, how will they be able to make this meaning credible for their children? This is the case for the father of a seriously anorexic girl. He would frequently let his daughter find him, right in the middle of the afternoon, naked, watching porn on the television. What is particularly striking about this scene is the total absence of veils with which the father exhibits his enjoyment. We must also be clear about this case: it is not the father's enjoyment in itself that is harmful for the daughter, but its blatant manifestation without any screen, which forces the daughter to introduce the Law of castration through anorexia, insisting the father pay a different kind of attention to his daughter's body. In this case, the preliminary intervention as far as treatment was concerned was that of demanding that the father respect the Law of the word, which forces the adult's sexual enjoyment to not incestuously involve that of their children. In this way the analyst attempts to reintroduce a respect for the Law that this father showed he did not have. The apparently prescriptive operation of the analyst ('avoid exposing your naked body to your daughter whilst watching porn!') has as its aim the submission of paternal enjoyment to a Law that transcends it. How can this father demand that his daughter apply herself at school and have a positive relationship with her own body if he projects an image of himself as a body that enjoys without symbolic filters (naked in the middle of the day) before the dumbfounded gaze of his daughter? In this case, the anorexia is unleashed following a dance recital in which the daughter is paralysed by the paternal gaze, unconsciously finding herself occupying the very position of the women in the porn films her father used for his own masturbatory arousal.

An adult must never be asked to represent an ideal of a so-called moral life, nor that of a complete one, but to *give weight to their own word*, which means trying first and foremost to *take on the consequences of their actions*. An adult is not held to embody any ideal of perfection, only to give symbolic weight to their own word. And this means showing their own children how they are themselves dependent upon a Law – the Law of the word – that stands above them.

## A New Discontent of Youth

Psychoanalysts once considered the crisis of adolescence to be a psychological manifestation of the pubescent storm that transforms the child's body into that of a young man or woman. It was the spring awakening: how to inhabit a new body that is no longer that of a child, one that strongly manifests new needs and desires?

Today, the evolutionary blade places ever-greater distance between puberty and adolescence. The age of puberty seems to be increasingly early, with children of ten, eleven years old behaving like real adolescents, whilst, conversely, adolescence seems to stretch way beyond puberty, appearing never to end. This evolutionary lag indicates another, more profound contradiction that makes the condition of our young people unsustainable in many ways. On the one hand, they find themselves thrown into a world dripping with information, knowledge, sensations, opportunities to meet, which goes well beyond the capacities of their mental age, but, on the other, they are abandoned by adults on their educational journey.

No other era has known individual and mass freedom like ours, like that experienced by our young people. However, this newfound freedom does not correspond to any promise for the future. The older generation has deserted its educational role, thus consigning our children to a mortally wounded freedom. The persistent offer of new sensations is multiplied, almost managing to remedy the dramatic absence of life prospects. Here we have an important aspect of the new discontent of youth. On the one hand, our children are exposed to a constant bombardment of stimuli and their freedom appears limitless, whilst on the other, adults avoid the educational duty symbolically imposed on them by the generational difference, whose function today would be, if possible, even more precious than in the past, when education was guaranteed by the force of the big Other of tradition. I remember my old elementary school teacher who had a habit of unbearably regurgitating a depressingly well-known educational metaphor: 'You are like vines that grow crooked, curved, curled up on yourselves. You need a pole and wire to bind the vine and make you grow straight. For you I will be that pole and that wire!' In the time that preceded the protests of 1968, the role of education was interpreted as a way of suppressing the very twists, anomalies and defects that make life unique. Today, however, this terribly repressive botanical metaphor no longer guides (thank goodness) the educational discourse. Today we no longer (thank goodness) use straight poles and steel wire to correct the twists and turns of life. The problem has instead become that of an absence of care shown by adults towards the new generations. What we are faced with here is the shattering of every educational discourse, believed by the hyper-hedonistic ideology to be repressive and something to liquidate as soon as possible. It is, if you like, the flipside of Foucault's perspective: the Other of control is weakened to the point where it dissolves and throws the new generations into a world without Law.[14] Not that adults are not, on the whole, concerned with their children's future, but this concern does not in any way coincide with taking care of them. Today's parents are, in fact, acutely worried, but this worry is often not capable of offering any support to their children's education. Our time is marked by a profound alteration in the processes of symbolic filiation between generations. On the one hand, like a sort of reverse Oedipus, it is the fathers who kill their children, who do not make space for them, who do not know how to fade, how to delegate. They do not provide opportunities, nor do they care about the future. On the other hand, the fathers do not want to stop being children, they do not want to miss a thing. They do not assume the symbolic consequences of their word.

Our children's lives are exposed to an unveiled knowledge, not only the traumatic knowledge referred to by the anorexic girl with regard to her father's nudity, but also that related to the adult world, once impenetrable to every demand and today reduced to a kind of unhappy piece of Swiss cheese. Children know everything about their parents, even that it would be best they did not. The alteration of the relationship between generations is also a product of this: children have access to boundless knowledge with no cultural mediation, knowledge that can be obtained without any difficulty (like that available on the Internet), in the same way they become their parents' confidants and a repository for their troubles. Rather than leaning on their parents, they follow, for the most part dumbfounded, the adolescent lives of the very people who should be taking care of them. Awaiting them is the cumbersome responsibility of decision-making, as their lives are no longer connected to the unchanging rails of tradition and familial transmission. It is, as Bauman would say, the liquid condition of the new generations. Less and less they find themselves following in the footsteps of their family members and increasingly they find themselves (for better or worse) obliged to invent their own path for growth. Our children exist in a time of mass freedom, in which isolation grows exponentially, along with conformism. Their responsibility grows prematurely, but it is increasingly rare that they are able to find, in adults, credible incarnations of what it means to be responsible. Take politics, for example; should this not be a 'lofty' cultural reference point to which young people can turn with confidence? But has the very place of politics (for Aristotle the highest and most noble of the arts was that capable of unscrambling individual difference for the common good of the *polis*) not itself been transformed into a crazed, adolescent party?[15]

Contemporary hyper-hedonism has excommunicated the adults from their educational task, left as something for moralists only. As a consequence, freedom now means doing whatever you want without ties or debts. But in the meantime, the debt grows and has submerged our lives, while the absence of the meaning of the Law has extinguished the generative power of desire. Freedom does not provide any satisfaction but is increasingly associated with depression. It is something we encounter with much greater frequency in today's young people. But why? They have all these opportunities, more than any generation that has gone before them, and yet they are depressed? How can we explain this? It can be explained by the fact that their freedom is, in truth, a prison, because it is a circus of enjoyment without any possibility of a future, of work, of fulfilment. We raise our children in playful confusion while history invests them with an enormous responsibility: that of making a possible future exist once more.

## The Trauma of the Non-Existence of the Sexual Relationship

When we listen to adolescents recount their failures in amorous initiations and the torment these provoke in them, the real of the non-existence of the sexual relationship emerges with all its traumatic potency.[16] Not that adults are spared this encounter. On the contrary, the betrayals, the abandonment, the pains of amorous ties, the losses appear traumatic for the human because they make manifest the irreducible core of the non-existence of the sexual relationship. All of this is amplified in adolescence, because it is the age in which we meet the Other sex for the first time, in all of its entirely incomparable heterogeneity. The little boy would have been happy wearing his father's Inter Milan shirt and the little girl would have been satisfied playing at dressing her dolls up like her mother. The time of childhood is a time sealed by the idealized identification with one's own parents. It is with the pubescent storm that this idyll is interrupted. What shirt will I wear on my first date with the girl from school? Which dress will I wear to meet him on my first date? Obviously neither football shirts nor Barbie dresses will be of any use here. We will be alone with no excuses before the thrilling and anxiety-provoking encounter with the Other sex. But this solitude – which arises from the lack of an instruction manual, and which, for the human, cannot be provided by instinct as we are all subjugated by the Law of the word which distorts that instinct – is destined to be doubled by the lack of symmetry that characterizes the encounter between the sexes. Every ideal of fusion, of specular identification, of identification with the Other, which often gives form to adolescent love, is destined to break up on impact with the hard kernel of the non-existence of the sexual relationship. This is a structural fact. Achilles will never reach the tortoise, the enjoyment of One will never be the enjoyment of the Other. The encounter between the sexes remains exposed to an incurable dissymmetry. I can never reach the Other as Other, I can never make similar to me that which is different to me. I cannot cancel out the difference between the sexes. No matter how many sexual relationships I will have, my body will only enjoy itself, it will only enjoy its own organ. I will never be able to absorb the body of the Other. The female demand for love is nourished by words, letters, poetry, lack. This condemns the phallus to impotency as an instrument of enjoyment, because it will never be able to offer her the sign of love. The tortoise looks beyond Achilles' virility, it wants something else, it searches the point of lack in the Other. Achilles will never be able to make her his own, as the feminine implies heterogeneity, difference, the impossibility of bringing the Other to the One. A traumatic void is thus left in the place of the sexual relationship. The male will have to learn that no sexual relationship will ever be able to abolish the otherness of the female body, whilst the female will have to learn that the phallus cannot infinitely respond to her demand for love.

The spring awakening of adolescence brings with it the eroticization of the Other sex, but also the tendency, through falling in love, to actualize its difference, to assimilate one with the other, to make a couple, to give life to a bond that cancels out the difference, the trauma of the non-existence of the sexual relationship. But in that very place where adolescent love culti-vates the dream of a fusion between the One and the Other that leaves no remnants, the encounter with the non-existence of the sexual relationship forces an often-traumatic awakening. This is why any interruption of this fantasy of unification is experienced with upset and pain. Whilst the non-existence of the sexual relationship is not a historical fact but continues to accompany the difference between the sexes, we can nevertheless say that there was a time when shortening the distance from the Other sex seemed a monumental task, and when the construction of the fantasy preceded the actual encounter with sexuality and the Other sex. Sexuality was fed by an imaginary wait, which eroticized the real encounter of bodies. Currently, however, the distance between the sexes seems to have been reduced. This is not only because girls (as happens with boys) now also separate tenderness and love from sex and the enjoyment of drives as a matter of course, but because, rather than feeding the fantasies of unification and the totalizing bond of falling in love, the encounter with the non-existence of the sexual relationship tends instead to produce a cynical exorcism of love, which is depicted as a trick, an illusion to do away with, a mask to let slip at the first possible moment. Sex is, therefore, used like a drug, as an enjoyment linked to a (partial) object collected from the body of the other, like a pure anaesthetic to reduce the pain of existence. The drive is no longer guided by erotic fantasy, structured through the unconscious fantasy. Now it acts without filters, de-eroticized, as a passage to the act, a simple urge to enjoy. The body takes on the status of just another product among many others.[17] Young men who conduct sexual relationships as if they were simply physical exercise, young women who sell their bodies for a mobile phone top-up. The difference between the sexes seems to have been abolished, but without the promise of emancipation. A compulsive sex life in both young women and men serves to prevent the loving encounter with the Other sex, and to keep the traumatic spectre of the real non-existence of the sexual relationship at bay. Today, this tends to detach young people from the myth of love in order to concentrate on the headless nature of the drive. The human partner (the Other sex) thus leaves space for non-human ones (drugs, alcohol, computers, one's own body image, food, etc.) that allow the drive to satisfy itself without passing through the unpredictability of the encounter with a human partner.

The adolescent can react to the encounter with the non-existence of the sexual relationship by denying the importance of the sexual reality (intellectualism, asceticism, conformism), or allow themselves to be pulled, transported into the chaotic vortex of drive without desire or eroticism. From this point of view, asceticism and unbridled consumerism are the two prevalent versions of the adolescent Super-Ego. What both these versions are trying to avoid is the trauma of the non-relationship. The difficulty in subjectivizing the encounter with the non-existence of the sexual relationship can spill over into a refusal to maintain an emotional and erotic bond with the Other, as every other form of bond appears threatened by this non-existence. The compulsive recourse to sex uncoupled from love, alongside other experiences of drive-led enjoyment that exclude the presence of the Other, aims to avoid the traumatic and anxiety-inducing encounter with the non-existence of the sexual relationship. Even fantasies of jealousy, so frequent and intense in certain adolescents, can display the wound of the lack of symmetry between the sexes and aim to reduce the object to the exclusive property of the subject. As if in order to protect oneself from the trauma of the non-existence of the sexual relationship it were necessary to incentivize an enjoyment capable of discarding the encounter with the Other sex in any way possible, such as through the traumatic enjoyment of drugs, food, alcohol, violence, sexual abuse and so on. In male sexuality, this anxiety-filled refusal of the trauma of the non-existence of the sexual relationship can also lead to the femicidal act.

## *Femicidal Violence*

The Law of the word, which is the Law of Culture, always constitutes a barrier to the exercise of violence. The Nazi official Goebbels felt an irresistible urge to reach for his gun every time he heard the word 'culture'. Violence against women is a particularly hateful, unbearable form of violence because it destroys the word as a fundamental condition of the relationship between the sexes. We notice that rape, torture, femicide, abuse of all kinds to which women are subjected, abolish the Law of the word. These acts are committed in the mindless, brutal silence of the drive, or with humiliating verbal insults and aggression. The Law of the word, as the Law that unites humans in reciprocal recognition, is shattered. The Law of the word, as we have seen, confirms that the humanization of life implies an experience of the limit and otherness. When this limit is surpassed, there is destruction, hate, anger, dissipation, annihilation of oneself and the other. For this reason, the condition that makes love possible as a wholly human form of bond is, as Winnicott theorized, the ability to stay on our own, the ability to accept our own limit. When a man, old or young, rather than interrogating themselves about the failure of their own love lives, rather than mourning for that which they have lost, or measuring themselves by their own responsibility and solitude, pursues, lashes out, threatens or kills the girl or woman who has abandoned them, they demonstrate how, for them, the bond was in no way founded on reciprocal solitude, but enacted as a phobic protection against the anxiety of solitude. We know that many young men who commit rape come from families where instead of the Law of the word, there is a sort of imaginary Law of the clan, a symbiosis between its members that paranoiacally identifies the outside as a place of ever-present threat.[18] The passage to the violent act that tragically concludes a relationship demonstrates how that emotional union was not made up of two solitudes, but was based on the anxiety-riddled refusal of solitude, on the furious refusal of the limit, on the trauma of the non-existence of the sexual relationship. Not on the Law of the word but on its negation. To claim a right of absolute ownership (of life and death) over one's partner is never a sign of love but, as Adriano Sofri reminded us, its 'profanation'.[19] In this claim, extreme narcissism is mixed with a profound depressive sentiment: I cannot bear not being everything to you and so I will kill you because I do not want to recognize that I am, in fact, nothing without you. To kill oneself after having killed everyone else: the world ends with my life (narcissism), but only because without yours I am nothing (depression).

Nothing tramples the Law of the word in such a hateful way as sexual violence. Human sexuality should be an erotic passion for the encounter with the Other, but its transformation into purely drive-led subjugation of the Other dehumanizes the woman's body, reducing it to a pure instrument for one's own enjoyment. The consensual nature of the encounter is ruptured by obscene vandalism. The eroticism of the deserted, annihilated body. However, we must not limit ourselves to condemning the bestiality of this violence. Femicide does not exist in the animal world. Here we have something more thorny that touches the human being itself and, in particular, the structure of the male sexual fantasy. A woman for a man is not only the embodiment of the limit, but also the embodiment of that which can never be disciplined, subjugated, wholly possessed, of which jealousy can only provide, for men, a vague awareness. This is why Lacan clearly distinguished between the modes of male and female sexual enjoyment (Achilles and the tortoise). Whilst the first is centred on having, on its ability to be measured, on control, on the performance principle, on the appropriation of the object, on its serial multiplication, on the 'idiocy of the phallus', the second appears to be without measure, unable to be reduced to an organ, multiple, invisible, infinite, not subjugated by the phallic obstacle. In this sense, female enjoyment is radically 'hetero'. It is an enjoyment that, on principle, eludes the mirage of phallic mastery. In each other's company, men exorcize the encounter with this 'infinite' enjoyment, Other from its phallic counterpart, by declaring all women to be whores. However, they do so merely as a phobically defensive way of protecting themselves from that which they do not understand and are unable to control. Adorno and Horkheimer said this in their own way in *Dialectic of Enlightenment*, when they drew comparisons between the woman and the Jew: both figures who cannot be ordered according to the phallic law of rigid uniformity because they have no boundaries. They do not obey the principle of identity, because they are always other than themselves, radically and truly *heteros*.[20] It is when faced with the vertigo of an enjoyment that knows no master, like that of the female body, defined by Lacan as Other enjoyment, as an enjoyment that is anarchic, nomadic, eccentric, not entirely subjugated by the Law of castration, that male violence explodes as a crazed, pathological attempt to colonize a territory that has no borders. It is clear to the psychoanalyst that this violence, even when carried out by men considered to be socially 'powerful', does not express only the arrogance of power, of the strong towards the weak, but is generated by a profound anxiety, by a veritable terror of that which it cannot control, of that insurmountable limit that a woman represents for a man. This, when it exists, is the beauty and joy of love, not reciprocal unification, not the mirroring of one's own power in the other, not the confusion of the one with the other. For a man, loving a woman is truly an endeavour that goes against his phallic nature, it requires him to be able to throw himself into the void. It means loving the *heteros*, the Other as totally Other, it means being able to love the Law of the word. For this reason Lacan believed that love, as such, as love for the other, for *heteros*, is always love for a woman.[21]

## The Technological Object and Depression in Young People

Depression should be something that accompanies a life that is passing, a life that is losing life, that is ageing, that is getting closer to death. Clinical psychoanalytic experience teaches us that this is not the case. Today, depression is overtaking the world of young people in the form of widespread inertia, a lack of enthusiasm, a tendential decline in desire. It is not true that young people do not have passion, enthusiasm, plans, but it is true that the expression of their discontent has changed. Whilst in the Oedipal time this took the form of an open transgression of the Law, of rebellious objection, antisocial rejection, today it takes that of a non-vital switching off of life.

If adolescence is the urge to have our own desire, for it to no longer be accommodated by the demand and satisfaction of the desire of the Other, as occurs in childhood, our time is characterized by the massive obstruction that is the object, which obscures the opening to desire. If desire is the transcendence of the object, an erotic opening to the Other, our time switches off this urge, encouraging the deadly enjoyment of the object. Whilst Oedipal adolescence was marked by the unconscious fantasy that demonstrated the centrality of the scopic drive (access to sexuality, for example, would happen through the filter of the unconscious fantasy), now the greed of the oral drive is at the forefront. The body of the Other is consumed without the filter of fantasy that structures the desire. Consequently, sex is used but is stripped of any eroticism.

Depression in youth signals the subordination of the strength of desire and its awakening to the presence of the non-human object. The body of drives, which should be the expression of a new force (puberty), appears to be switched off. The depressive experience is, in fact, the experience of existence as pure weight: glaciation, passivization, the reduction of the subject to an object. When depression occurs in youth, something is opposing the smooth running of life, something withdraws from the open sea of life, something grows sad. Take, for example, the addiction to the technological objects that seems to have flooded the world of today's youth. It is a fact: connection to the Internet, rather than strengthening the connection to life, can replace it. Of course, it can sometimes amplify the connection to life, but it can also bring about a disconnection. The unconscious itself, which is actually fed by the desire of the Other, ends up being replaced by the technological object. The virtual nature of this bond replaces the erotic impact with the body of the Other. This is the false promise of the technological object. What is the nature, however, of the Freudian object? If we take little Ernst's spool as our example, this object appears to be the product of an absence.[22] The Freudian object always occurs against the backdrop of a void. This is because it is only against such a backdrop that the game of desire becomes possible. The technological object, however, always appears as a phagic surface that swallows the subject. If the Freudian object is constituted by the symbol, if it is an organization of the void, if it circumscribes the void, the technological object plays an anti-depressive, medicinal role because it tends to occlude, to fill the void. And yet in order to play the game of desire you must be separated from the Thing, the void must be produced. The game of desire can only happen against a backdrop of a sublimation of loss. Is the Internet made of void? In one sense it is an opening, possibility, the world. In another it risks becoming a substitute for the world.[23] It can become a perpetual connection that generates a disconnect from the Other and isolation, it can create a hypermodern version of the unconscious. It is an articulated and limitless knowledge at the subject's disposal and an alternative to that of the body. A knowledge that creates a distance from the erotic encounter with the Other; contacts seem to multiply, but in reality they remain virtual. In the same way, the technological knowledge our young people avidly stockpile remains clearly separated from the truth, split from the experience of the Law of desire.

The case of a boy I saw in treatment is emblematic of this. He is a subject that was sequestered away from a psychotic and deeply depressed mother during his infancy. Only his father was able to carry the boy with him, educating him in the ways of the discipline and exertion of farm work, proving to him that a world did exist that was different from the maternal one. But when the boy found himself alone with his mother, he felt as if his body was sinking into a fusional vortex. He felt himself elevated to the position of an idolized object, pure fetish. The maternal depression gave him the strong impression he was his mother's only 'lifesaver'. This perception symbiotically reinforced their relationship: he slept with her, as she would sing him to sleep and curl up next to him. They played, exchanging snot and saliva. Their bodies seemed to be melded together, liquid, one mixed with the other. They would lie embraced on the marital bed, from which the father had always been exiled. Saved from psychosis by the presence of a father capable of transmitting the positivity of work and the libidinal investment in life, it is in adolescence that this boy develops a particular symptom. He is unable to pass his driving test. He makes his first girlfriends come and pick him up. He makes himself, as he himself put it, 'always be carried by the Other'. His first love is for a girl to whom he dedicates himself entirely, reproducing the same symbiosis that had characterized the relationship with his mother, who, in the meantime, had died. This first love lasts two years, and when it ends the boy falls into a profound depression. He isolates himself, he feels lost. He dedicates his life exclusively to the technological object (the computer), which becomes his only partner. He spends hours in front of his computer screen. This continual connection is, in reality, a form of disconnection from the world. The object is not constituted by the symbol (as happens with the Freudian object), but impedes the symbolization of mourning, resuscitating the incestuous morbidity of the uninterrupted presence and discontinuity of his mother.

The encounter with the analyst is the event that reconnects him to the desire of the Other. In this way, by working on the particular linguistic bond with the maternal voice during his sessions, he will discover poetry. His interest will draw him towards a poet writing in dialect who forges linguistic forms that favour a language imbued with body and affectivity. This language is similar to infant lallation; the *lalangue* of the poet recalls the *lalangue* of the mother. Now the object can return to its background of absence, becoming the object of a new sublimation. The ever-present object, like the extension of the phagic presence of the mother, dissipates in the rhythm of the words and their musical charm.

This brief clinical sequence demonstrates how the only connection that counts, the only one that invades and moves life, is that of the encounter with the desire of the Other. In another clinical case recounted by my colleague Aldo Becce, the protagonist is a boy who has been living for a few months in the isolation of his room.[24] There is no transmission of desire in his family: the boy describes his father as an 'ectoplasm' and his mother as an 'absent presence'. For this boy, the attraction to videogames takes the place of the hole left in symbolic filiation. The analyst's first move is to ask the boy if he too can play the game on his computer. In this way the boy is able to experience there being someone other than him that can win. He is not condemned to win on his own because always winning, winning on your own, is really a way of losing, as it makes the very game of desire simply impossible. You can never really play any game if you already know you are always going to win. This is the theme of the didactic dream of one of my obsessive patients, who finds himself torn between two women: the ideal love of his youth and the adult woman expecting his child. The dream is the following: the patient is playing poker with friends. Each time he is dealt four winning aces. No one wants to play with him any more. So he goes to a casino, but again he continues winning and this stops him from playing because no one wants to play with him any more. The inevitability of victory stops him from finding other players ready to face him. What this dream highlights is that the impossibility of losing – the narcissistic refusal of symbolic castration – produces a much more catastrophic loss than that he would have experienced had he stopped always winning – the loss of the very possibility of participating in the game of life, the game of desire.

But let's return to Aldo Becce's patient. The analyst's intervention introduced *the relationship* to the boy's autistic rapport with the technological object. In this way, enjoyment without the Other guaranteed by the object is forced to interrupt itself, and thanks to this interruption, the boy will try to use it in new ways, for example to message others. After the entrance of the Third, the very object that had previously imprisoned him is able to become the tool with which to counter his social isolation. Thanks to the possibility opened up by playing alongside the analyst, by playing the Other, the Internet goes from being an autistic game to being a bridge with which to connect to the world. These are brief glimpses into treatment allowing a new transmission to be realized, for the same object to appear differently; *are we dealing with an object that plugs a void or an object that establishes a connection with the Other through the void?* Whilst the Internet certainly can isolate from the Other, it can also allow the establishment of new contacts and forms of connection with the Other. In this case, the analyst's work culminated in the socialization of the technological object, making it a version of the Other, breaking the subject's narcissistic closure and making a symbolic transmission of desire possible.

This case teaches us how perpetual connection and disconnection are part of the same pathological position. Without the alternation between connection and disconnection there is no subject. The right to be disconnected is as important as that to be connected. In this case, it was the intervention of the Third (against the background of a real father who was 'ectoplasmic') that modified the picture, and that, through transfer, allowed for the animation of a subject who appeared dead. This animation occurs by virtue of there being a new version of the object. The subject detaches from the object in order to invent new uses for it, thanks to their connection to the desire of the Other. It is, in fact, this connection (that to the desire of the Other) that makes all others virtuous. Nevertheless, the possibility of the game implies the production of a void, and so a disconnection from the continual presence of the object. This is what our time seems to deny: silence, the suspension of time, the right to be disconnected. The boy is only able to access a new use for the technological object when he allows the Other (the analyst) to insert himself between the boy and that same object, producing a separation between subject and object. He disconnects from the object thanks to the Other and this allows him to reconnect in a more satisfying way.

## *Evaporation and Invention*

In the time of the father's evaporation there is not only the urge for mortal enjoyment, but also a greater possibility for invention: the void of the father is not only a bottomless abyss, but also the opening up of new possibilities. It does not only contain the risk of the compulsive drive towards deadly enjoyment, but also the possibility of paths that are no longer linked to the normative weight of tradition. This is another reason why we must not harbour nostalgia for the father-as-master, father-as-totem, father-as-pope or father-as-hero who has the final word on the meaning of good and evil. This evaporation can potentially clear the way for invention. If there is the evaporation of the father, there is (as Lacan would say) the 'forced choice' of invention. Freud's reflections on the youth of Leonardo da Vinci can be used to illustrate this new condition. Freud insists on reminding us that Leonardo was not initially recognized by his father and was raised by two women: his mother and his maternal grandmother. This is the basis for Freud's broader thesis, which seems to contrast with the structuring value that he attributes to the Oedipal complex: Leonardo's extraordinary creative impulse and drive to research would not have been possible had he not learned to 'renounce his father'. This thesis opens itself up to a vision of inheritance that transcends the blood tie. Leonardo is mis-recognized by his real father, but he is able to transform this absence of inheritance into a new possibility. He is, as demon-strated by the etymology of the term 'heir', orphaned by his father and, for this very reason, an heir. The father's absence seems to lighten life, as if the act of waiting for the father were substituted by scientific research as a possibility to rediscover in Nature and its Law the symbolic dimension of the Law of the word.

Freud writes:

In most other human beings – no less today than in primeval times – the need for support from an authority of some sort is so compelling that their world begins to totter if that authority is threatened. Only Leonardo could dispense with that support; he would not have been able to do so had he not learnt in the first years of his life to do without his father.[25]

In the time of the father's evaporation we are obliged to be a bit like Leonardo. It would be interesting to ask ourselves what the relationship is between the child-as-Telemachus and the child-as-Leonardo. If, as we will consider in the next chapter, the heir's condition is etymologically that of the orphan, of the missing, of the wilderness, then we are all heirs without a kingdom, heirs who must (as happens to Leonardo) renounce their father. Freud guides this renunciation towards a new subjective responsibility. The evaporation of the father can become a condition for invention only if the *renunciation of the father* becomes something very different from the *refusal of the father*. The heir does not relinquish their responsibility or their relationship with the Other. Freud sketches a portrait of this figure when, following Schopenhauer and the teachings of his patients, he introduces the death drive – the human tendency to enjoy beyond all limits, to enjoy even the death of their life. Unlike Schopenhauer, however, he does not choose the path of ascesis, he does not suggest abandoning the world or propose the nirvanization of life as a remedy to this drive. Rather, he introduces the subject of responsibility. But what does it mean to pose to oneself the problem of responsibility starting with the evil of the death drive? What does it mean for one to consider the problem of responsibility starting not from the Ego, as suggested by post-Freudian psychoanalysis, but from the Id, from the subject of the unconscious? Is this not a problem we encounter in the contemporary discontent of youth? How can I be free without destroying myself or going crazy? How can I fulfil an enjoyment that potentiates life rather than dissipating it? How can I associate desire with enjoyment without losing myself in the 'night of the Proci'? Lacan, following in Freud's footsteps, shows that the time of desire is *always* a time that implies the risk of losing oneself, of getting lost, of alienating oneself from a regular, conformist, ordinary administration of one's own life. In every experience of desire there is something that refuses to adapt to the reality principle. But what is the fragile frontier that separates one from acting in favour of one's own desire and losing oneself, throwing oneself away, consuming oneself? Is this not the frontier that each must cross when they take on the limitless and unique responsibility of their own desire? There is, in fact, no limit established by the Other that defines the point to which it is 'right' to push for the fulfilment of one's own desire. We can only evoke and inhabit the uncertain frontier that separates the enjoyment of the Proci from that capable of bringing about satisfaction, that distinguishes between deadly enjoyment and the surplus enjoyment derived from the acting in favour of one's own desire.

Freud, in an unprecedented move, once placed the responsibility for the relationship with the unconscious, when he asked himself whether or not we are responsible for our own dreams.[26] What does it mean to take responsibility for something that transcends us? What does it mean, as happened to Leonardo, to learn how to renounce one's father not because one is creative but in order to be creative? This is the same problem Freud tackles in 'Some Reflections on Schoolboy Psychology' when he states that the problem with educating the young can be summed up in the task of realizing a 'detachment from his first ideal [...] his father'.[27] Is this detachment not the greatest and most dangerous task of inheritance? Rightful inheritance can only exist when we recognize our provenance from the Other, the symbolic debt that binds us to the community of speakers and mortals. The only condition for realizing this detachment is that we be inscribed in the Law of the father as the Law of the word: separation, discontinuity, being mistaken all have as their requirement the foundational experience of belonging, despite a 'detachment from the father' being the most authentic thing at stake in every inheritance. Odysseus returns, but only to let go, to allow for the separation to take place and set in motion the most radical mourning of his person. Only now are we ready to call upon the figure of Telemachus as that of the 'rightful heir'.

## 3

# From Oedipus to Telemachus

*Four Kinds of Child*

In this chapter we will examine four kinds of child: the child-as-Oedipus, the Anti-Oedipal child, the child-as-Narcissus and the child-as-Telemachus. The first two are long-standing protagonists of Freudian psychoanalysis. They are used as prime examples of children. The first comes from a period that extends until the end of the 1970s, accompanying the long wave started by the great protests of 1968. The second is a consequence of the first. The Anti-Oedipal child would like not to be in conflict with the father but to be without a father, to be radically orphaned. But this child misses the point that the rightful heir can only ever be an orphan. Their will to self-affirmation would want to be free of any bond with the Other, but that will end up fomenting an incestuous enjoyment that yields to the death drive.

The child-as-Narcissus sums up the period of the so-called 'reflux' that has characterized the last few decades leading up to the great economic crisis that has overwhelmed the West. This crisis, together with a series of transformations that have profoundly affected our collective life, force the entrance on stage of a new protagonist: the figure of the child-as-Telemachus. With this figure I would like to propose a new way of reading the current relationship between parents and their children. Whilst, with the child-as-Oedipus, conflict, struggle, the clash between two generations, between two different ways of understanding the world has dominated, central to the child-as-Narcissus is the indistinct assimilation of parents with their own children, that confusion between generations, the absence of conflict and the cult of an individual happiness without ties to the Other. The child-as-Telemachus, however, is a new interpretation of the current discontent of youth. Telemachus is the symbol of the rightful heir: he knows how to be a child and how to make the most dangerous of journeys in order to be an heir. He shows us how to be children without renouncing our own desire.

## The Child-as-Oedipus

The child-as-Oedipus is a child who, as in the myth recounted by Sophocles, lives in a state of abandonment. The Oracle warns King Laius that his son will be ungrateful and will kill him. In order to defend himself from this prophecy the king entrusts the child to a servant with the order to end its life. Moved by compassion, the servant does not carry out his task and saves the child's life, a child who, raised in total ignorance of his provenance, finds himself, a strong, young man, involved in a disagreement at a crossroads. At the centre of this disagreement is right of way: *who goes first?* The young man

93

challenges the rich man who demanded to be given the right of way guaranteed to him by generational difference to a duel and kills him, without realizing he was, in fact, his father. Oedipus goes on to become the king of Thebes and husband to Jocasta, Laius' wife and his own mother, with whom he has children, the obscene fruit of incest. Tiresias, the blind prophet, reveals to him the hidden truth of his history. Overwhelmed by pain, Oedipus gouges out his eyes and abandons his land, an exile.

From this myth Freud carved out the Oedipus complex as the 'nuclear complex' of neuroses. Oedipus' desire reveals human desire to be driven by an incestuous tendency. What does this mean? Why, as Lacan also states, should this be the most decisive, most radical word used by Freud to describe the nature of human desire? Desire is not just a demand for the presence of the Other, an appeal, an invocation of the Other to save us from the dark night, but is also the frenzy to possess everything, to have everything, to know everything, to be everything. Incestuous frenzy, pushed to deny the existence of the limit, to refuse the impossible inscribed in the very heart of the human by the Law of the word. And yet it is only by virtue of this Law that life can be humanized and transcend the closed world of animals. The Law of the word is not just that which forces life to constitute itself through its appeal to the Other, through the demand for love that opens and exposes the One to the Other, but it is also that symbolic Law of castration that forces life to lose the maternal Thing. This is what Oedipus rejects, slipping instead into the tunnel of ruinous enjoyment. This is why parricide and incest are the 'criminal' representation of his desire, which is structured as a 'complex' only insofar (as Freud demonstrates) as it implies a fundamental triangulation, the one that exposes him to a traumatic impact with the Law that occupies the location of the Third with regard to the perverse couple of mother and child. The object of desire (the body of the mother) appears symbolically forbidden. Oedipus' tragic destiny is that he can only reach the meaning of the Law of castration *after* having committed his crimes. This is where his guilty conscience comes from, leading him to the dramatic gesture of blinding himself, followed by self-imposed exile.

There was a time in which conflict between parents and children could be read through the paradigm of Oedipus. The child-as-Oedipus is the one who challenges the older generations to a fight to the death in the affirmation of their own desire. At the centre of the Oedipus complex is the conflict between the Law and desire, between reality and dream, between the old and the new. The time of the child-as-Oedipus has been the tragic time of conflict between generations: children against parents and parents against children. The right of way claimed by the older generation is not recognized by the new, ungrateful one. Children harbour a desire for the death of their own parents. Oedipus is the hero of destiny and the father is nothing more than a repressive obstruction of his hunger for freedom. The child-as-Oedipus sees the father as an obstacle to the fulfilment of his satisfaction. The Law of the father establishes itself as an unbearable barrier to his desire. The child-as-Oedipus sees this Law as an irreducible antagonist in the anarchic dimension of the drive. In this sense, it was he who inspired the great protests of 1968 and 1977: the children who demanded the possibility of a new world against their parents, and the parents who reacted by denying their children their rights.

There is a structure and a supra-historical dimension to the Oedipus complex that we are loath to discuss. The incestuous tendency of the unconscious desire and the conflict between generations – between the established order and the transcendence of desire – define, as far as psychoanalysis is concerned, human life itself. This is not the point I wish to highlight. Rather, I would like to demonstrate how, in our time, the paradigm of the child-as-Oedipus is no longer capable of explaining the relationship between parents and their children. One of the current problems afflicting this relationship is, indeed, the failure of the dimension of conflict and the difficulty this necessarily implies. In place of this conflict we have a confusion of generational difference and, consequently, a profound alteration in the process of symbolic filiation. What is the point then? It is that the real crime of the child-as-Oedipus is not their conflict with the older generations, because in this necessary conflict they can find their symbolic placement in the chain of generations, but the will to disavow their provenance, the wanting to eradicate any trace of the Other from themselves. To put it in clearer terms: *Oedipus does not know how to be a child*. He would like to deny any form of dependence on, or symbolic debt to, the Other. He would like to deny his own status as a child, just as the Other, in the myth, denied his responsibility as a father. This is why Freud views the Oedipus complex as a paradigm of neuroses. The neurotic is someone who laments being without inheritance, not having received anything. They are someone who incessantly reproaches the Other for not having given them their due, that which it would be their right to have, without, however and at the same time, being capable of truly receiving anything from the Other, unable to bear being indebted to the Other, without managing to accept their condition of being a child. In order to inherit from the Other it is necessary to recognize oneself as lacking, as an orphan, deprived of one's own sense of self. The neurotic thus cultivates the dream of their total autonomy from the Other, despite the fact that everything they do has the intention of making the Other exist in order to avoid the ethical responsibility that invests them as a subject. The neurotic hates the father-as-master but cannot be without him, because without this father, without this blind hate towards their father, their life would be threatened by non-sense.

Oedipus' error is not the claiming of his dream as a right, but having misunderstood the Law, experiencing it only as an obstacle on the path that leads him to the fulfilment of his own desire. This brings with it the reduction of his freedom to pure opposition to the Law, which ends up feeding the myth of desire as a liberation from all limits. In this sense Oedipus is, paradoxically, already carrying the seed of the Anti-Oedipus. The Anti-Oedipal child would like to escape the Law, do away with the Law, make the Law of the word a thing of the past, they would like to free themselves from such concepts as 'limit', 'castration' and 'Name of the Father'. Like the child-as-Oedipus they experience the Law only as a repressive nightmare. As such, the

Anti-Oedipal child lives in Oedipus' heart, but he cannot see who he is, he does not know how to be a child, and is unable to accept either his provenance or the truth of his unconscious desire. Oedipus' greatest mistake, which he will only truly be able to recognize at the end of the tragedy, is that of having been opposed to the Law of the word, misunderstanding its meaning, and of having seen the Law as nothing but a trick.

## *The Anti-Oedipal Child*

What does it mean when we say that the child-as-Oedipus carries within it the seed of the Anti-Oedipal child? The explicit reference here is to the Anti-Oedipal culture developed in the 1970s following the publication of a ground-breaking text: *Anti-Oedipus* by Deleuze and Guattari (1972). It offers the strongest possible criticism of psychoanalytic practice and theory from the left. Today, as we are well aware, it is conservative, right-wing criticism that rages against psychoanalysis. Its practice is disparaged in favour of scientific psychology, the chemical power of psychiatric drugs, the exclusive authority of psychiatry in the treatment of mental health problems. However, the authors of *Anti-Oedipus* – a philosopher who was already well regarded and a brilliant psychiatrist who had been in analysis with Lacan, before dramatically breaking all ties with him – do not reprimand psychoanalysis for not being sufficiently scientific in its theoretical affirmations and clinical practice, but for something far more radical. They reproach it for being in the service of the established order and the powers that be. Their accusation is that, having discovered the 'unconscious desire', psychoanalysts deliberately downplayed the revolutionary potential of this discovery, placing themselves at the service of the master. What would the psychoanalytic cult of Oedipus hold itself up with if not blind obedience to the repressive and mortifying Law of the father?[1] This book mobilized the revolt of an entire generation, my own, the class of 1977. It theorizes a political critique of psychoanalysis that does not so much promote an improbable alternative theory to that posited by psychoanalysis (so-called 'schizoanalysis'), but a veritable theory of revolution in which anything is possible. Many young people of my generation lapped this idea up enthusiastically, myself included.

Foucault had declared that our century would be Deleuzian. He was right, but in a sense that was probably rather different from the way he had hoped. Deleuzism got away from Deleuze himself (as is often the case with 'isms'). *Anti-Oedipus* unwittingly gave rise to an unconditional approval of the revolutionary character of desire *against* the Law, which paradoxically ended up colluding in the dissipative orgy that has characterized the flows, not of the desiring-machines as Deleuze and Guattari had predicted, but of money and enjoyment that have fed the crazed mechanism of the capitalist discourse in the age of its financial globalization. Lacan had tried to point out the danger of this to the duo. In an interview he gave to *Rinascita* in May 1977, in which he was asked for his opinion on *Anti-Oedipus*, he responded that 'the Oedipus [complex] in itself constitutes such a problem for me that I do not believe that what Deleuze and

Guattari have chosen to call the *Anti-Oedipus* could be of any interest whatsoever'. Lacan warns that one should not be too hasty to pull the trigger on the father. The revolutionary juxtaposition of the desiring-machines and the Law, of the impersonal and de-territorializing urge of the power of desire and the conservative tendency to the rigid territorialization of power and its institutions (Church, Army, Family, Psychoanalysis) risked dissolving the ethical sense of subjective responsibility. For Deleuze and Guattari, the word 'subject', like the word 'responsibility', should be banned along with 'Law', 'castration', 'lack', 'Name of the Father'. The Anti-Oedipal child worships unequivocally the mindless force of the drive, which, however, causes them to slide fatally towards a view of the human that tends towards vitalistic naturalization (and is a bit fascist). Take, for example, the recovery of the Freudian concept of Id. For the Anti-Oedipal child, the Id is the expression of the anarchic power of the body that enjoys everywhere, beyond all limits, beyond all Law: 'It is at work everywhere, functioning smoothly at times, at other times in fits and starts. It breathes, it heats, it eats. It shits and fucks.'[2] From this perspective the Law of castration would only function as a protective and inevitably repressive screen against this free energy of the body of drives. Conversely, the Lacanian reading of the Freudian Id preserves the centrality of the ethical category of responsibility. The Id is the place of a thorny truth – that of my unconscious desire – which it is up to the Subject to assume or otherwise. It is not a case of liberating the natural and impersonal power of the Id, but of translating this power into the call made to the subject by the unconscious desire, giving it the task of occurring in the place in which its vocation, its wish (*Wunsch*), manifests itself. Whilst the Anti-Oedipal child shits and fucks all over the place, making fun of the Law of the word, Lacan insists on asking the subject what they have done with the transcendence of their desire, to position the subject as always responsible for their position.[3] What have you done with your desire? Have you made this transcendence the source of satisfaction, of fulfilment of life? Have you known how to do anything with it? Or have you avoided the encounter with the real of this call? Have you pretended it never happened? Have you closed off your ears? Have you run away from this impossible task? Have you been scared? Have you wanted to ignore the unconscious call of your unconscious desire, choosing the neurotic path of repression or the psychotic path of foreclosure?[4]

While the liberation of flows of desire rightly reacts to the fatalistic cult of the reality principle, to which psychoanalysis seems to have devoted itself, it does not seem to realize it is creating a new monster: the myth of schizophrenia as the name of life that rejects any form of limit, of the free life of the father, life freed from the Other. The myth of the 'schizo-body' as an anarchic body, a body in pieces, full up, 'without organs', constructed as a machine of drives that enjoys anywhere, the irreducible antagonist of the Oedipal hierarchy, has been translated into the flows of the cynical and perverse machine of the capitalist discourse.

And yet reading it again today, Deleuze and Guattari's *Anti-Oedipus* is also much more than this. It is not just the celebration of a desire that is not capable of reckoning with the Law of castration. There is a more subtle thread that runs through it, one which my generation has probably failed to fully grasp. It is a significant theme, if not the book's central one. Deleuze and Guattari reformulate it using the words of the psychoanalyst Reich, a great theoretician of mass psychology, fascism and character analysis, before he began raving about organic energy: "'Why did the masses desire fascism?'" This is a problem we also find in Spinoza: "Why do men fight *for* their servitude as vehemently as though it were their salvation?'"[5]

In *A Thousand Plateaus*, published ten years after *Anti-Oedipus*, Deleuze and Guattari have to return to the opposition between desire and the Law with a clarification that should have been taken more seriously. Beware micro-fascisms, beware the micro-Oedipuses who install themselves precisely where we thought there was nothing but the liberating flow of desire. 'The mother', they write, 'feels obliged to titillate her child, the father becomes a mommy.'[6] How this self-criticism seems to anticipate our own time, in which the desiring-machine has transformed itself into a machine without Law or repression of the capitalist discourse! Just as Nietzsche sagely warned those embracing the liberating announcement of the 'death of God' of the risks of creating new Idols (scientism, ideological fanaticism, atheism itself, every kind of fundamentalism), Deleuze and Guattari warn their 'children' that an insidious danger is inscribed in that same theory of desire as an infinite flow, like a 'line of flight' that constantly oversteps the limit, like a perennially de-territorializing power. Be careful, they seemed to tell us, 'that this line does not turn into destruction, pure abolition, the passion for abolition'. Be careful this 'line of flight' that rejects the limit does not become a 'line of death'.[7]

## The Child-as-Narcissus

In this time dominated by the evaporation of the father, in which the balcony of St Peter's stands empty and the memory of the secretary general of the Communist Party has vanished (Nanni Moretti), and Ideals seemed to have all been defaced (Pasolini), a false horizontality seems to have substituted for the rigid hierarchy that once guided our collective life. Narcissistic specularity seems to have gradually taken the place of the generational difference and the conflict this inevitably fuels. Children have taken the place of parents. Not only because, as has rightly been noted, the child has bent the family order to their own narcissistic demands. Rather than adapting to the symbolic laws and the times of the family, the child-as-idol demands the family mould itself around the arbitrary law of its whim. But, in particular, because our time, by unilaterally emphasizing the universal rights of the child, ends up viewing with suspicion all action that takes on a vertical responsibility for the child's education. As if reiterating the centrality of the educationally responsible action meant automatically returning to a nostalgic disciplinary and authoritarian model of education rather than understanding the need expressed by the child to be helped to form itself as a subject, to be able to become a subject aided by the actions of the Other! Is this not the reason

Françoise Dolto proposed replacing the word 'education' with 'humanization'?

The time of the father's evaporation is the time of the evaporation of adults. The child's narcissism depends on that of the parents. If a parent takes the carefree happiness of their children as a benchmark for their educational action, leaving to one side the transmission of desire and the subjective obligation that this transmission brings with it, the parent's action fatally evaporates in their support of the children's whims. They are thus relieved of the anxiety of having to embody the limit, but their children are potentiated in their narcissism, unable to tolerate any experience of the limit. Even the 'desire to have a child' is no longer necessarily associated with that of taking responsibility for their education, their symbolic adoption. Today, the narcissism of men and women often searches for the real experience of filiation – becoming a mother or father – as a whim made possible by the progress of medical science, which allows us to artificially do away with the contingency of the sexual encounter and the trauma of the non-existence of the sexual relationship, allowing us to do everything on our own without passing through the symbolic mediation of the Other.

If a parent's task is to exclude the encounter with the obstacle, the encounter with that which cannot be assimilated, with injustice, from their child's experience, if their concern regards how to flatten any bumps in the road so as to avoid an encounter with the real, the adult ends up raising a child-as-Narcissus who will remain forever imprisoned in an entirely specular version of the world. As such, the passage of the child-as-Oedipus to the child-as-Narcissus that lies at the centre of the sociological formulations of Gilles Lipovetsky, revisited in a psychoanalytic context by Pietropolli Charmet, is not simply a passage that liberates the new child from the torment of guilt and punishment that afflicted the old child-as-Oedipus.[8] The absence of any guilty conscience is never a good sign in psychoanalytic treatment.[9] The real point is how to provide an interpretation of the guilt that is not simply morally super-egoic. If guilt originates in ceding, renouncing, abandoning one's own desire and the responsibility implied by its singular assumption – the only guilt deemed Lacan worthy of this name – the child-as-Narcissus appears without guilt not because they have fulfilled the Law of their desire, but because this Law is at risk of not being inscribed in any way in the subject's unconscious. It is because, even more radically, the subject appears to be without desire. In my opinion, it is not a case, therefore, of over-emphasizing the passage from Oedipus to Narcissus as a liberation from any guilty conscience, but rather of grasping how this passage risks a failure of the generative power of desire, which continues to exist (albeit within the tragedy of deadly conflict) in the child-as-Oedipus in the form of the demand to subvert the reality principle represented by the father's authority. In this sense, as Lipovetsky and Pietropolli Charmet also note, the myth of self-generation is more rightly the myth of the child-as-Narcissus.[10]

The cocoon that protects the child-as-Narcissus would like to save them from the pain of existence. We must not forget that every educational action, even the most correct and loving one, can never expect to save our own children from the encounter with the real without any sense of its existence, from its limitless contingency, from its absolute anarchy. What does this mean? It means that we can till the fields, sow the best seeds, shelter the first shoots from the harsh weather, cure their disease, ensure the right amounts of light and water, but all of this, and all the other things we would do, will never be able to tell us what the result will be. We can help to prepare fertile ground, but nothing can guarantee the effective fulfilment of this fertility. Life is exposed to the irreparable risk of contingency without any protection. Of course we know that the transmission of desire from one generation to the next, from parents to their children, is the strongest way of preventing life's tendency to become dispersed in deadly enjoyment, to vanish in the 'night of the Proci'. If there has been an effective transmission of desire, a subject will always be able to respond to the morose sirens of deadly enjoyment and their call by resorting to the invisible treasure of their own desire. Conversely, when desire is left to languish, when its transmission has not been effective, when its inheritance is lacking, it will be easier for life to be dazzled by deadly enjoyment. This transmission (the transmission of desire from one generation to the next) is undoubtedly the adult's most important educational task. But the time of the child-as-Narcissus is a time, as I have said, in which adults have evaporated. The evaporation of the father brings with it the evaporation of the symbolic weight of generational difference, the difference between parents and their children, and, in the last instance, the very existence of adults. The child-as-Narcissus is not, therefore, only the child authorized to cultivate the dream of their own fulfilment and happiness, but also the child without desire, plastic-coated, apathetic, lost in the phagic world of objects, unable to bear any frustration. They are the little vampire-king, unmoved by the efforts of the Other and their own symbolic debt.[11] It is a fixation with the myth of Pan (which, by no coincidence, means 'all') that excludes any experience of the limit and lack. This is the destiny of the child-as-Narcissus: to remain hooked on a perennially youthful image of themselves, subtracted from the symbolic incision of castration, eternally vital. The relationship with their own image is extended in a specular way into that with objects. In this relationship there is no subject. It appears as if submerged by a timeless enjoyment. The 'night of the Proci' knows no pause, no break, no rhythm. It is the continual enjoyment of a diffuse multitude, of a formless herd without subject or responsibility. It is the inconclusive enjoyment, deprived of any desire, of getting by, wasting, living without desire.

## The Child-as-Telemachus

In Homer's *Odyssey*, Telemachus is the son of Odysseus. His father is forced to abandon him in order to leave for the Trojan War. He will remain alone in his home for twenty years. The sea and its hidden dangers prevent the hero's return to the island of Ithaca, but Telemachus awaits him steadfastly. His house has been invaded by young princes, the Proci, who ransack the food supplies, rape the female servants, force

Laertes, Odysseus' father, to take refuge in the countryside. They behave like arrogant masters in a house that is not their own. Their greatest ambition is to marry Penelope, the wife of Odysseus. Telemachus is forced to watch all this impotently. He tries to take various initiatives to save his land from the violence wreaked by the Proci. He asks for help from the people's assembly and undertakes a dangerous journey (during which the Proci plan to kill him) in search of news of his father. Finally, when Odysseus does return to his land and meets Telemachus in the humble home of the swineherd Eumaeus, the son will not be able to recognize his father, whom the goddess Athena had wisely transformed into a beggar in order for him not to be identified by his enemies. Only later will the two finally be able to embrace one another and bring their implacable justice to the island, getting rid of the Proci one by one.

Telemachus' wait is not the wait for an anonymous Law, but the wait for the routine application of the Law of the Code. He awaits the return of a father. His desire is the desire for the 'father's return': 'If men could have anything for the asking my first wish would be my *father's* return', declares Odysseus' son.[12]

As children, we have all been Telemachus. We have all waited for a father to return from the sea. Telemachus' gaze watches the horizon, he is open to the future. My thesis is that our time is no longer under the sign of Oedipus, of the Anti-Oedipus or Narcissus, but of Telemachus. Telemachus demands justice: in his land there is no longer Law, no longer respect, no longer symbolic order. He insists on the re-establishment of the Law and that the 'night of the Proci' be brought to an end. Unlike Oedipus, who falls flat, blinded, or Narcissus, who only has eyes for his own reflection, Telemachus looks to the sea. His eyes are open and trained on the horizon, not gouged out, blinded by the guilt of his own criminal desire, nor fatally seduced by the allure of his own sterile beauty. Telemachus, unlike Oedipus, does not see his father as an obstacle, as the place of a hostile Law of drive. He feels no conflict with his father. He, as we will soon see, is the rightful heir. He awaits his father, he awaits the Law of the father as that which will be able to re-establish order in his house, now usurped, offended and ravaged by the Proci. He searches for his father as the place of a possible just Law. Telemachus, unlike Oedipus, faces his father's absence with the hope of seeing him again. On the one hand, we have the child-as-Oedipus and the fight to the death with the father, and on the other, the child-as-Telemachus who desperately searches for a father. It is without doubt, at least to my mind, that today's young generations are more akin to Telemachus than Oedipus. They ask that something act as a father, that something return from the sea, they ask for a Law capable of bringing a new order and a new horizon on the world.

Psychoanalytic treatment demonstrates how the empirical, de facto absence of the father is never a trauma in itself. This absence becomes traumatic only if it implies a symbolic absence. This is one of Lacan's classic theses. Not one of Odysseus' relatives goes mad on the island of Ithaca. The absence of the father is not signified by Penelope's word as an irresponsible abandonment. Odysseus has not abandoned his family, he has not abandoned his people. They say that he has been lost at sea. The paternal absence becomes traumatic, Lacan would say, if the mother's word interprets it as a sign of disinterest, as a refusal of the symbolic adoption that the choice for paternity imposes. The word of the mother has the power to signify the father's absence in entirely different ways. For this reason, Lacan bases the symbolic value of the Name of the Father on the word of the mother. This word will signify the father's absence either as a guilty act of negligence or as a necessary act that allows the family to live. The absence of the father is not traumatic in itself, this entirely depends on how it is symbolically transmitted by the word of the mother. How does Penelope transmit the Name of the Father? She communicates to Telemachus that his father's absence is not a whim, that it is not the result of a refusal of his paternal role, nor of cynical selfishness. With her wait for Odysseus, Penelope communicates to Telemachus that his father's absence is laden with human meaning. Her vigil keeps the Name of the Father alive. Signifying Odysseus' absence as the 'absence of a presence', she transmits to Telemachus the full meaning of his inheritance as a son.[13]

In this case, absence does not mean the trauma of abandonment, but drives the necessity for vigil, for waiting and for prayer. It is no coincidence Lacan makes these three dimensions of human experience (waiting, vigil and prayer) models with which to decipher the figure of desire as the desire of what lies Beyond, as desire of an Other Thing.[14] Desire cannot be crushed by the mere satisfaction of needs, but reveals itself to be different from animalistic yearning precisely because it is driven by a transcendence that opens it up to that which is new, to that which is not yet known, to that which has not yet been thought, not yet seen. In this sense, Telemachus carries with him an aspiration that transcends the simple presence of things. His desire is not simply a nostalgic desire for his father to return, but that there should be a 'father', that there should be a human meaning of the Law and not just an animal one, that there should be a Beyond, an Other Thing with regard to the incestuous enjoyment of the Proci and the devastation of his home. Telemachus' desire is a desire for an Other Thing. Not for an Other world, a utopian reality that does not exist or an ideal city that would be impossible to reach. Telemachus demands justice now! His indignation refuses the current situation, not in the name of an impossible ideal but in the Name of the Father. What does this mean? He defends the particular dignity of his family, his loved ones, his land, his mother and his city. He does not make an abstract appeal to the right of the heir, to the universal right of Kingdom. His indignation is moved by this attack on the people he loves. He does not invoke an abstract Law, but a justice that might protect his home. He is in search of human meaning, not of the juridical meaning of the Law. He is looking for the meaning of the Law of the word, the Law trampled by the Proci.

In the *Odyssey*, the adolescent's world is represented simultaneously by both Telemachus and the Proci. The latter are, in fact, Telemachus' peers, young princes like him. But their youth tramples the Law of the father, humiliates his people, declares Odysseus dead, depriving him of any form of respect. The scrapping of the father happens violently. Parricide and incest trample the dead father who will no longer return, desecrate his memory and take his wife. Is there a greater crime than this? The Proci are a Sadean version of Oedipus. They refuse the Law that forbids incest and respect for the paternal Law that represents it. They trample the unwritten Law of hospitality that, in the Grecian world, is the most profound incarnation of the Law of the word.[15] They want the queen to marry one of them so they can take Odysseus' place and stop Telemachus from inheriting his father's kingdom. They do not recognize the Law that limits enjoyment. *The death of Odysseus is the death of the Law* because it authorizes incest and murder. Only the goddess Athena saves Telemachus from the bloody hand of the Proci, who had ordered a deadly ambush against him upon his return from the journey in search of news on his father's fate. The prayer, waiting and vigil of Telemachus, his gaze open on the sea, invoke the father not as an obstacle (as happens with Oedipus), but as the possibility of bringing back the Law of the word to his own house and city. Telemachus is in the position of the *desiderantes*, just as Julius Caesar describes them in *De bello gallico*: he survived the battlefield, he is not dead and he is waiting for those who still risk their lives under a starry sky, without a single star that can guarantee the return of their companions. For Lacan, vigil is a name of desire, its own special version because it always transcends the object as a simple presence.[16]

Whilst Oedipus' discontent causes a fight to the death with his father and a crime consisting of parricide and incest, and that of Narcissus is produced in a suicidal mirror, for Telemachus discontent is living in a world where the human sense of the

Law of the word is insulted, offended, humiliated. Whilst for Oedipus the Law is a brake on desire and the father an adversary whom he casually meets along his path, for Telemachus the Law is that which can lead the devastating chaos of deadly enjoyment to the necessary experience of castration and desire. In the first case, incestuous desire comes into conflict with the Law, whilst in the second, desire invokes the Law as a possibility.

Telemachus, unlike Oedipus and Narcissus who are without-name, is nourished by the Name. Alongside Penelope he makes the Name of the Father exist. In this sense, he is following in Jesus' footsteps. It is the son who makes the father exist. As Lacan states concisely, it is Christ who saves God.[17] God's faith is only cemented around the sacrifice of the son. It is the son's testimony (of the Word that is made flesh in the Gospel according to John) that provides the basis for the father's existence and gives structure to that of God. The same thing happens in the great theological subversion depicted by Cormac McCarthy in *The Road*. Here, it is the surviving existence of a child in a world ripped apart by violence and horror, in a world without God, without the Name of the Father, which makes God's existence still possible. A father's love for his child, being greater than that for God, is not portrayed here as a sin (according to Augustine, sinning was loving the creature more than the Creator), but becomes the only condition to make faith in God's existence possible once more.

The father-protagonist in *The Road*, who does all he can and more to protect his son's life from Evil, is, in reality, saved by his son. As long as there is a child, there is the possibility of human life, the possibility that the Law of the word will return to regulate a world that has fallen into the abyss of the absolute violence of deadly enjoyment. In the same way, as we have noted, when in the *Odyssey* Odysseus has to present himself, he does not do so as king of Ithaca but as 'the father of Telemachus'.[18] What does this mean? It means he chooses not to present himself through the appearances of power (as the ruler of a kingdom), but through his ethical responsibility, through a responsibility that precedes all legitimacy. He is a 'father of', not a 'proprietor of'. It is the Name of the Son that defines him, not the Name of the Father. At the forefront here is the limitless responsibility of a father rather than the power of his Name. It is the same responsibility that urges him to return home. It is in order to remain faithful to this responsibility that he is also able to renounce the thrill of roaming and the immortality of the eternal. In fact, the greatest sacrifice Odysseus makes is that of the dream of immortality promised to him by the seductive Calypso. What motivates Odysseus to renounce the dream of immortality? He is only able to do so thanks to the power of love. There is something that takes Odysseus beyond the absolute, beyond the promise of the eternal, beyond the mirage of a life's salvation from its own end. It is Penelope's face, ravaged by time, it is the life of his son and his community that are worth more than immortality and personal glory.

My lady goddess, do not be angry at what I am about to say. I too know well enough that my wise Penelope's looks and stature are insignificant compared with yours. For she is mortal, while you have immortality and unfading youth. Nevertheless I long to reach my home and see the day of my return.[19]

Where does Odysseus find the strength to detach himself from the sleep of an enjoyment that promises to be immortal? I do not believe this is simply a question of iron will and self-discipline. Odysseus here is not that different from Abraham, who, by following a seemingly opposite path, gives up Isaac to the wilderness. It is not as Lévinas believes: Abraham and Odysseus are not in opposition with one another.[20] Odysseus' return is not a re-appropriation of his own essence, it is not a return to the Same. Odysseus has in no way preserved that which is his own. Upon his return he will find Penelope and his beloved son. He will find the memory of a love and the land of his fathers. But he will find all of this having lost it. No one will give him back his wife's youth and the smiles of his son as a child. His return does not take the shape of a second enthronement. He will be forced to undertake another journey before finding peace. The One is never reconstructed. Instead Odysseus demonstrates the irreplaceable power of the loved object, its absolute incomparability, the strength of staying faithful to one's own desire. He demonstrates how the eternal is in the world, it is here, it lies in the bond with those we love. It is not just nostalgia (*nostos*) that afflicts Odysseus. His is rather a 'faithfulness to the land'. We must not place a moral value on the content of Odysseus' choice (his return home, his fidelity to his wife and child), but demonstrate how he chooses to return as a response to the Law of his desire, to hold Penelope close to him, to recognize his son, to bring the Law of the word back to his community. Not because these are universal moral values but because they make his life worth living, satisfying, happy.

What Abraham and Odysseus have in common is their love for the son. It is this love *à fond perdu* that drives their decisions; that of Abraham to lose Isaac, to give him up to the desert, and that of Odysseus to forsake his own immortality in order to return home, to recognize Telemachus and rediscover the face and body of Penelope, to rehabilitate the Law of the word. From this perspective, even the celebrated reading of Odysseus proposed by Adorno and Horkheimer in their *Dialectic of Enlightenment* appears fatally partial: Odysseus is not only the name of 'sacrifice', the self-preserving strategy of reason when faced with nature. The logic that inspires his life is not just that of the astute control and self-dominion that 'survives only at the cost of his own dream'.[21] Rather, Odysseus indicates the path taken by the father who chooses, *à fond perdu*, out of love for his child and his wife. He chooses to obey the Law of his own desire, a Law that goes beyond any sacrifice. His renunciation is not made in service to his domain and appropriation, but in service to his desire and its symbolic transmission.

# 4

# What Does It Mean To Be a Rightful Heir?

## Inheritance as Reclamation

In his unfinished final work, entitled *An Outline of Psychoanalysis*, the father of psychoanalysis' last word is purposefully dedicated to the theme of inheritance. Freud cites one of Goethe's famous phrases: 'What thou hast inherited from thy fathers, acquire it to make it thine.'[1] The act of inheritance is defined here as a *reclamation*. In order to inherit something from the Other, to truly be an heir, it is not enough to passively receive an inheritance that has already been constituted. Inheritance requires a subjective movement of recovery, of the subjectivization of the debt. Without this recovery of the past that constitutes us, without this temporal redoubling in which we must make ours that which has already been our own, in which we must repeat precisely that which has constituted us, there can be no subjective experience of inheritance. Inheritance never occurs as a natural law, out of destiny or historical necessity. It is not an obligation but rather implies a bond, a symbolic debt. If inheritance is a subjective movement of reclaiming one's own having-been, it does not simply define an event of descendence, but is the very material from which the reality of subjective existence is made. Human beings, as speaking-beings (as, Lacan would say, 'parlêtres'), are above all heirs of language, heirs of the Law of the word. This is the symbolic debt that binds them to the Other. This is another reason why inheritance is under no circumstances an income. An heir is not the person who collects wealth or genes from the Other; the authentic inheritance is not made of blood or biology. It is that which Christ tried to explain to an astounded Nicodemus: if you truly want to be born, your first birth, your biological birth, is not enough. You must be born a second time. Not from your mother's womb, Jesus explains calmly. The second birth, which concerns the problem of inheritance, is a triumph of subjectivity. This means that the first birth, that of flesh and blood, is not sufficient to render life human. Life is not humanized by receiving its genetic dowry or the economic assets to which it has a right, but by truly making its own that which it has received from the Other, subjectivizing its provenance from the Other, the symbolic debt that binds us to it. Even if we only inherit a dead body, its ashes, its corpse, even if we were to inherit 'shit',[2] this would not mean we could, as Heidegger would say, go without choosing our inheritance.

For Lacan, biological life is only humanized by passing through the desire of the Other. In order to be reborn, as Jesus invites the philosopher to be, the yeast of desire is needed. The encounter with the desire of the Other is necessary. This encounter is never guaranteed by ancestry, nor by the historical memory of the past. An inheritance is never an appropriation of oneself, but always has as its premise a separation, an uprooting, a distance that is impossible to fill. For this reason

Heidegger poetically affirmed that existence is a 'creature of distance'. The reclaiming of inheritance is never a 'making one's own' in the sense of self-appropriation, of homogenizing, of softening the improper otherness of the Other, so much as a recognition of our provenance and the symbolic debt that this implies. Inheritance is not the appropriation of an income, but an ever-moving reclamation. Inheritance therefore coincides with existence itself, with a subjectivization of our existence that is never fully complete. We are nothing more than the stratified totality of all the traces, impressions, words and meanings that, coming from the Other, have constituted us. We cannot speak about ourselves without speaking of the Other, of all those Others who have determined, fabricated, produced, marked and fashioned our life. We are our word, but our word would not exist if it were not constituted through the word of others who have spoken to us. The Law of the word sanctions the existence of this symbolic debt at the origin of the event of the word. The possibility of my word is given by the presence of the language that transcends it and on which it must be able to inscribe itself in order to exist in its singularity. The act of the word is always mine, but it is always mine only insofar as it reclaims in a singular way the universal existence of the Other of language. A life is nothing but this learning to speak one's own word through the word of the others.

Inheritance cannot, therefore, be the cancellation of this word and this memory of the Other, of the symbolic debt that binds us to it, but nor can it be its passive repetition. Inheritance, as Freud tells us using the words of Goethe, is the effect of a reclamation of that which has been. It is the product of a choice, of a subjective assumption of all of our history that is, first and foremost, the history of the Other.

## An Excess of Memory

The movement of inheritance – the reclaiming of inheritance – can always fail. Psychoanalysis shows two fundamental ways in which this failure can occur: one on the right and one on the left. The one on the right happens when inheritance is assimilated as the mere repetition of what has already been. If inheritance is a movement of reclamation, of making our own what is already ours, of wanting it again, of wanting it a second time, of being born symbolically, then inheritance cannot be reduced to a simple repetition of the past, a passive movement of absorption of that which has already been. Inheritance is not the reproduction of what has gone before. Rather, the past's repetition, the excess of identification, of attachment, of alienation, its passive absorption or its veneration are all ways in which inheritance fails. This is why Freud underlines how inheritance is, above all, a decision taken by the subject, a movement towards 'Reclamation'. This movement is the opposite of a nostalgic doubling-down. The 'reclamation' of inheritance means the subversion of the passive replication of the already-been. Inheritance is not cloning. It is never a passive reproduction of an ideal model gleaned from the past. Neurosis tends to interpret inheritance as repetition, an absolute fidelity to one's own past, the perpetual infantilization of the subject, dependence without differentiation, obedience without criticism, a monumental and archaeological conservation of the past. The heir's gaze never only looks back. In order to reclaim and therefore truly possess our own inheritance, we cannot linger too close to that which the dead person has left us.

## *The Anti-Melancholy of Jesus and Nietzsche*

I propose two scenes that were crucial for my youthful understanding of what it truly meant to inherit. The first is a scene from the Gospel recounted by both Matthew and Luke. In Matthew's version, the problem is the relationship between the teacher and his disciples. One of them turns to Jesus and tells him: 'Teacher, I am ready to follow you wherever you go.' Jesus responds: 'The foxes have holes, the birds of the air have nests, but the son of man has nowhere to lay his head', reminding his disciple of the human status as a wanderer, without home, without roots – without inheritance as a solid identity. At this point the disciple asks for permission to go and bury his father. And Jesus, even more resolute, responds: 'Let the dead bury their own dead', forbidding his disciple to participate in his father's final farewell. Jesus takes him by force, shaking him, recalling him with a determination that always appeared excessive to me, merciless, shocking. 'Teacher, let me first go and bury my father', the disciple asks meekly: 'Follow me! And let the dead bury their dead',[3] the teacher answers with inhuman steadfastness. In Luke's Gospel we find an additional comment on this scene, in which he quotes Jesus as saying the following:

'No one who puts his hand on the plough and looks back at things is fit for the kingdom of God.'[4]

This scene is about the movement of inheritance. Jesus invites us to leave the dead to the dead, to leave the dead to those who are already dead. This is where his mercilessness lies. He appears to obstruct the act of mourning, which, as we know, requires a certain lapse of time in order to be carried out. Jesus, however, invites us not to retreat into the past, he allows no time, whereas for Freud, mourning requires extra time, it demands 'time and energy' in order to be carried out. Is Jesus' word here not perhaps a radical alternative to that of psycho-analysis, which goes against any decisional activism, teaching us the importance of knowing how to stay with the loss, to give death the necessary time needed for its effective symbolization? Do we not need, as Freud said, the correct 'lapse of time' for the loss to be processed mentally?[5] Do Jesus' words not then seem to invite a maniacal fleeing from death, a rejection of completeness? That would be a deceptive reading of his words. What must be highlighted in this scene is the dense fabric that binds memory to forgetting. We are given what I believe to be a correct interpretation of this scene, or rather I would be given it during my time as a young student some years later, by reading Nietzsche's work *On the Uses and Disadvantages of History for Life*.[6] What is at play in this text? Here we have a special illness, a hypertrophy of memory: *historical illness*. What does it consist of? Nietzsche interrogates himself on the disadvantages and uses of history for life. He asks himself whether the thought of the past (its antiquarian or monumental worship, or its critical rejection) can become damaging to life. The answer to this question assails the problem of inheritance. When historical knowledge, the knowledge of the past, does not serve life but enslaves it, we do not have inheritance but an illness of inheritance. An excess of memory stupefies, crushes the present under the weight of the past, making the future impossible. An excess of history makes it impossible to begin again because it harnesses the present to the yoke of consolidated tradition, subjecting it to the weight of a memory that becomes an archive and monument. This is historical illness! Memory, the retreat into the past, drains life and makes the future of the kingdom impossible. When the thought of the past becomes an incessant rumination, there is lethargy and a depressive fading of life. This is Nietzsche's theory. But it is also Freud's: the act of mourning *passes through* death, but is not crystallized around it. Is this, ultimately, not also the thesis put forward by Jesus? Let the dead bury the dead! If life allows itself to be trapped by loyalty to the Other of the past, to the Other of tradition, to its Law, to the archives and monuments of the past, it will provide no possibility for creation, it will give no inheritance. For Nietzsche this is the pathetic, melancholic obesity of the historical: a truly historical life, however, needs to forget, it needs the suspension of memory, to be 'non-historical', to separate itself from the past. It is the same paradox that we find in Freud: the memory of our past is fundamental, but it can give rise to a melancholy fixation that ends up rescinding the plasticity of the drive. It can drive an experience of the past as an ideal, leading to its narcissistic idealization. This is the melancholy choice: to remain caught on one's own past, to refuse the experience of separation, to insist on the fixed adhesion to a lost object, to reduce inheritance to the passive and infinite repetition of what has already been. This is why Jesus admonishes his disciples: 'Let the dead bury the dead!', 'Do not look behind with one hand on the plough!' Kin must never consume life; life needs separation ('Do not think I have come to bring peace on Earth. I did not come to bring peace, but a sword';[7] 'Who is my mother? And who are my brothers?'[8]). For Nietzsche, it is a case of practising non-historical vertigo, the vertigo of separation. The plastic force of mourning consists in this exercise of memory that allows us to reach a state of forgetting that is different from the one that would like to cancel out the past. It is not a case of wanting to forget, of not wanting to remember, it is not repression. Rather, it is a way in which those hoping to find the ideal for their own life by adjusting their past can lay down their melancholy yoke. It is a case of *being in history, but without history*. Jesus warns us of the dangers of not being able to forget. Does the experience of memory strengthen or weaken life? Is it useful to life or harmful? Melancholia is remaining attached to the lost object, not moving forward, not wanting to move past death. The melancholic subject is assailed by the idealization of their past. But the veneration of the past is an illness of memory and it is – here is the point that we are really interested in highlighting – a failure of inheritance. Even Telemachus risks occupying a position of nostalgia, he risks the melancholic idealization of the great father, the father-as-king, the father-as-hero, as a lost father. In order to inherit, one must be trapped by neither the loss of the Ideal, nor the horror of the present. However, this is precisely what is happening with this generation of children who can see nothing before them, no horizon, no Ideal. Inheritance requires that which Lacan called the 'mourning of the father'. Otherwise we become professional heirs and the forward motion of inheritance is crystallized in a rigid identification with the ideal of the past. Even Telemachus risks resembling the tramps in Beckett's *Waiting for Godot*. What if the father was also the person who never actually arrives? The person destined to be lost at sea forever? Destined to leave us all alone, orphans, lacking. What if he were destined to abandon us?

This is why it is necessary to be born a second time, to break with kin ('Who is my father? Who is my mother? Who are my siblings?'), to leave one's home, to uproot oneself. To be born is to kill, it is to break the shell, to lean into limitless contingency, to exist in a radical discontinuity with everything that has gone before. Inheritance as reclamation implies, therefore, a time of separation from and forgetting of the past. It implies the bottomless vertigo of the non-historical. The historical illness is, for Nietzsche, the opposite of inheritance, an *idolatry of the past*. This can also be an idolatry of populations and civilizations. Life, however, not only needs the light of history, but also darkness, shadow, oblivion. Franz Kline theorized that it was necessary to have a sound knowledge of art history, that 'one cannot avoid seeing the past', but that in order to generate an artistic gesture worthy of that title it is also necessary to be able to forget everything that has gone before, otherwise an excessive love of the past will end up making it impossible for a personal style to emerge.[9]

When Freud speaks of inheritance as a reclamation he wants to show how inheritance is an open risk and not a consolidation of an already acquired belonging. Roots do not seal this identity, but must instead be recaptured from a wandering movement each time. This is why memory can never be consumed by inheritance. We need memory of the past, but only in order to reach, at its peak, a point of forgetting that makes possible a brand new, singular act capable of introducing new signifiers. Inheritance as reclamation is never unquestioning loyalty to the past, it is not an archive memory, not an income, but implies forgetting as a strength, it implies the strength of forgetfulness. Heidegger said that we always choose what we inherit. For this reason, the unconscious in Freud is not just a memory of the most archaic past, it is not just a depository for that which has been repressed, but it is also the locus of the strength of desire, of that which has not yet been realized and that asks to be realized. But what does it mean then to 'mourn the father'? Inheritance coincides with mourning as a labour, a labour of mourning. What is a labour of mourning? It is being able to bring memory to the power of forgetting; to forget the dead not because we have cancelled them from our life, but because we have made them our own and only in this way can we say that we have been able to forget them, that we have been able to let them die, to leave them to truly be dead.

## Negation of the Symbolic Debt

There is, however, another way in which inheritance can fail: that of the left. What does this involve? It involves cutting ties with the past, refusing memory, the cancellation of the symbolic debt that accompanies our provenance from the Other. Inheritance, as we have seen, is never consumed by the activity of memory, and yet without memory no inheritance can take place. The movement of inheritance is situated halfway between memory and forgetting, between loyalty and betrayal, between belonging and rootlessness, between filiation and separation. Not one against the other, but one in the other, one screwed into the hardwood of the other. Whilst the rightist failure of inheritance arises from an excess of loyalty to the past, this leftist failure happens because of a rebellious refusal of the past. It is the specular capsizing of veneration. The passage through adolescence often oscillates between these two extremes: an idealizing veneration of the past, a conformist identification with family models, and the violent oppositional rupture with the past, the negation of debt and the one-way demand for one's own (false) autonomy. This second extreme seems to characterize our time in particular, a time of a freedom that wants to be absolute and free of limits. The hypermodern veneration of freedom separates it from the responsibility of memory and the act that knows how to suspend it. It is a freedom that proclaims itself by rejecting the hard labour of mourning. Consequently, it is a freedom without responsibilities. This freedom upholds the illusion (to varying degrees of tragedy and farce) that the subject is somehow its own parent. This is the hypermodern cult of self-sufficiency and the refusal of any kind of dependency. Psychoanalysts are very familiar with the fact this refusal (the refusal to be children, the refusal of inheritance) brings with it nothing but damage and destruction. It is impossible to exist without the Other. Human existence is never self-sufficient, it cannot do without the bond with the Other. The myth of freedom without ties is a hypermodern mirage that fuels the perverse reduction of freedom, split from any form of ethical responsibility, to a pure will to enjoyment. The father's objection, the push to destroy the Name of the Father sticks, indebts forever. It does not allow for separation. This is the unconscious myth of all the Anti-Oedipal children. The failure of inheritance in this case takes the form of a demand for the destruction of the symbolic debt to the Other.

The Gospel parable of the killers in the vineyard lends itself as a demonstration of the criminal dimension of the refusal of inheritance and its catastrophic outcome. The farmers who rent the vines do not recognize the debt to which they have agreed. Not only do they refuse to pay what they owe, but they hit and offend the owner's servants, sent to collect the rent. And when the vineyard's owner decides to send his own beloved son (a symbolic allusion to the life of Christ is evident here), believing the farmers would at least show him due respect, he is killed mercilessly: 'But the tenants said to one another, "This is the heir. Come, let's kill him, and the inheritance will be ours." So they took him and killed him, and threw him out of the vineyard.'[10]

In this Evangelical scene there is no inheritance, just undue expropriation that occurs through the brutal killing of the heir, denying any form of symbolic debt. The killers in the vineyard are the epitome of the leftist failure of inheritance. The fantasy that moves them is that of an illegitimate appropriation of the Other's inheritance, a negation of the pact with the Other, of the symbolic debt that binds them to the Other, to the owner of the vines. Killing the son is like killing the father; it is the rejection of symbolic filiation in the name of a fantasy of self-generation.[11] But what sense does it make to still talk of symbolic debt today, when it seems as though the older generations have left our young people nothing? At a time in which the older generations have obstructed the horizon for the new generations, when they have left real debts in the place of symbolic ones, when they do not vacate their posts, when they do not transmit desire but doggedly defend only their own wicked privileges? What symbolic debt, at a time when the place of the Other appears entirely inconsistent? Does this new call to debt not sound moralistic and, more to the point, oppressive for the new generations? There must be no confusion here. Indignation and conflict do not exclude inheritance. To inherit means to recognize myself as inscribed in an order that I cannot govern. It means recognizing that my word always comes from the word of the Other; it means accepting our constitution as being deprived of foundations. It means attributing value to the Law of the word. It is no coincidence that believing oneself to be a whole Ego is considered by Lacan to be the mental illness *par excellence*, the maximum expression of human madness, the greatest madness. We are made of the Other, we come from the Other, we breathe the oxygen of the Other, we cannot exist without the Other. Of course, we also have the duty to separate ourselves from the Other; to be born is always, as we have just seen, also to kill. But the condition for a possible separation lies only in the recognition of our provenance, of our belonging to the Other, of the impossibility of being One without the Other.

The refusal of inheritance can take the path of obsequious and formal repetition of the past or that of its rebellious refusal. Subjection to the past without invention and freedom without ties or symbolic debt are the two ways, each the mirror image of the other, in which the endeavour of inheritance can fail. The proclamation of a freedom without responsibility or memory is the leftist way of failing inheritance. It is viewing freedom, like those killers in the vineyard, as unanchored from the symbolic debt that binds us to the transcendence of language.

## Telemachus Is the Rightful Heir

Let's go back to Telemachus. Why is Telemachus the rightful heir? How does the act of inheritance occur in Telemachus? The wait, the being *desiderantes*, does not consume his position in reference to his father. We have already mentioned how his vigil runs the risk of nostalgia. The Telemachus complex appears to have two souls: the nostalgic-beseeching one, and the practical-active one. Telemachus does not limit himself to waiting and invoking his father, but instead he acts. He rips himself from his wait, he sets himself in motion. The Homeric cycle of the 'Telemachy' recounts this action, this forward movement by the son. It tells the story of Telemachus' journey. He decides to go towards his father, to rediscover the memory of his deeds; he sails first to the lands of Pylos and then Sparta, before going to meet the old heroes of the Trojan War. He searches for his father's footsteps, he looks for news on his life. This journey, the one that every heir must make, is filled with danger. The Proci conspire to take his life and Telemachus is only able to escape them thanks to the intervention of the goddess Athena. During this journey, Telemachus is in danger because he confronts his past without limiting himself to simply receiving it as a guarantee, but by immersing himself in it to the point where he risks losing himself. Is this not perhaps the correct movement of inheritance? Does inheritance not always carry with it a danger of becoming lost? We must not forget that Telemachus the heir, like all rightful heirs, is an orphan, he is disinherited.[12] In his voyage to reclaim his inheritance he does not encounter his father because, in reality, an encounter with the father is never possible. The evaporation of the father dictates that the encounter with the father is never already predestined, but that it may happen, or not, only within the limitless contingency of life. More to the point, this encounter can only be retroactively signified. It is not the passing-down of genetic similarities or the continuation of a blood line. The encounter with the father is a possibility of our being children. In Homer's tale this becomes possible *only after Telemachus' journey*. It is only upon his return, having survived the attempt on his life, that Telemachus will be able to encounter his father in the hut of the humble swineherd Eumaeus, without recognizing him, initially at least. It is only *after* this journey that Telemachus will be able to embrace, and be embraced by, his father, in one of the poem's most moving passages.[13]

As Freud would say, using Goethe's words, what does Telemachus' journey teach us if not that inheritance is not already constituted at the Origin, but is only realized when the subject makes it its own in a forward movement, a movement of reclamation? It is only as orphans that the right kind of inheritance can take place. If inheritance means entering into a relationship with one's own past, if it supposes the recognition of our provenance and the symbolic debt that binds us to it, this never entails an appropriation of the Origin (the Hegelian reconnection with our own essence), because inheritance is not a consolidation of identity but, as Telemachus' journey demonstrates, a forward movement, an exposing of oneself to risk and danger.

## What Does Inheritance Mean?

It is the experience of the impossible introduced by the Law of the word that brings us into existence as children. The child is indeed that which comes from the Other. In order for the experience of the limit to be creative and not dissolve into a narcissism of frustration that glorifies it (an arrogance of humility), nor into a worship of desire without Law that gives rise to its Anti-Oedipal cancelling out, it is necessary this experience of the limit be linked to that of filiation. From this perspective, every human being is, in being a child, *an heir*. Every human being comes from the Other, inhabits language, is in a relationship of symbolic debt with the Other from whom they hail. In this sense, a filiation capable of being generative implies that responsibility be associated with freedom. The Other that welcomes life is an Other invested by a limitless responsibility because it renounces any claim of ownership over that life. But also because life that is welcomed is never life in general, but always *a life*, a particular life – that life, that name, that unique odour of the child. The Other's responsibility consists in the humanization of the event of life, in recognizing a life as human life, in translating the cry into a call. The limitless responsibility does not lie so much in the biological generation of life, but in saying 'yes!' to the human event of life. Filiation implies an act of symbolic adoption of life. Not of life in general, but of that life, that life that is wanted and welcomed in even its worst details. Because the apparition of a particular life is a drop in the ocean, though the sea is unable to absorb that drop. This is why Lacan states that love is always and only ever love for the Name. It is not love for life in general, but a love that is embodied by a detail, a body, a face, by the very Name of *one* life.

What do I mean when I say that our responsibility in the process of filiation appears limitless? Our responsibility to welcome life is limitless because the birth of each life alters the meaning of the world, changing it *forever*. If the Other manifests itself not as a welcoming but as a refusal, life is dissociated from meaning and falls into a state of total abandonment (*Hilflosigkeit*). In order to make itself human, life needs the present presence of the Other. Present presence means a presence driven by desire. If this encounter does not happen, life is exposed to a dissociation from meaning, it appears as life without meaning. This is what we regularly encounter in the treatment of depression. Life is only humanized through the oxygen of the Other's desire, through a care that is not anonymous, through the particularization of that care. But there can be no humanization of life without inheritance. Inheritance is the founding principle of all symbolic filiation. Inheritance is making mine that which has made me by recognizing the symbolic debt that binds me to the Other. It is subjectivizing my provenance from the Other, which is not simply a family tie, but a hailing from language, from the Other as the Law of the word. Filiation, implying the movement of inheritance, supposes that there is a transmission of desire from one generation to the next. Freedom without responsibility refuses filiation in the name of self-generation, or limits itself to offering nothing more than a caricature of being children, reducing filiation to the worship of immaturity.

## Recognition of the Symbolic Debt

So what is inherited? And what is inherited when the past is a dead body? When the father is a sadist, a father without love? When adults have evaporated? Inheritance does not imply a rediscovery of an identity that has already been constructed, of timeless roots, because it is a movement that goes beyond kin. We do not inherit a certificate of identity because there is no genetic inheritance. Being symbolic, filiation breaks up ancestral descendence. With inheritance I sink into my past not in order to rediscover my Origins, but to return once more, to emerge from them. This sinking is not, as Hegel thought, a rediscovery of identity in tradition. The movement of inheritance always implies being *children without fathers* in the sense that it is not so much a case of receiving from the Other, but of losing the Other. The authentic heir is always an orphan of the Other. This is what happens for Telemachus, who is moved to search for his father without having ever really known him. Homer's 'Telemachy' is, in fact, a search for the father that starts with his absence.[14] It is this movement that is most pertinent to inheritance. The father who presents himself as the embodiment of an omnipresent Ideal, as an exemplary model, makes any inheritance other than the reproduction of the Same impossible.[15] So what is inherited in the symbolic process of filiation? It is the possibility of desire. Desire is what is at stake with inheritance. We are, before all else, the word of the Other. We depend upon those words, they run through us. The application of the rule of free association, in psychoanalytic practice, demonstrates how by speaking of themselves the subject must speak about their Other. When they talk about themselves they are talking about the Other, they are talking about how the Other has spoken to them. There is no existence that is an *ens causa sui*. We are not masters of our own house, Freud repeats. So how can we understand this original expropriation of our foundations? How can we understand this absence of self-sufficiency that the hypermodern fantasy of freedom would like to destroy? The recognition of life's dependency on the Other, of our own symbolic debt, is the first condition for inheritance. Lacan speaks of 'constitutive addiction' in relation to life's symbolic debt towards the Other. Pathological addictions are instead driven by the narcissistic illusion of *going it alone*, doing without the Other. It is one of the most serious expressions of the current discontent of youth. It is a desperate attempt to cancel out the constitutive dimension of addiction.[16]

## The Symbolic Difference Between Generations

The fantasy of freedom tends to cancel out the symbolic difference between generations. The ideology of equality destroys the time required by life to make itself be, as Lacan would say. It destroys the generational difference and the limitless responsibility invested in the adult during the process of filiation. The child-as-Narcissus is coupled with parents-as-children. The adult's responsibility for the educational act is missing. No one wants to take on this burden. Where have all the adults gone? How can inheritance or symbolic filiation occur without the existence of adults? The Telemachus complex demonstrates that the demand made by the new generations is no longer that of transgressing the Law, but that there might still be respect for the Law of the word. That there might still be an adult capable of bringing testimony of the alliance between Law and desire. This is what we have called the passage from Oedipus-Narcissus to Telemachus: the current discontent of youth expresses a demand, an insistent invocation of the Law of the word.

As we have seen, inheritance is a movement that can fail, and this can happen because of an excess of identification with the Other, or because of an excess of rebellion towards the Other. Human life must recognize the symbolic debt, but it must not remain imprisoned by kin. The recognition of the debt favours and does not obstruct the separation from the Other. Obedience to the past, its cloning, and the revolt against the past, the refusal of the debt are two specular ways in which the interpretation of the Law of the word can fail. Over-identification with the Law, or the Law's rejection, are both simply super-egoic misunderstandings of the Law. Failure through cloning stops the act of separation from progressing. It is not able to do without the father. Failure through revolt, wanting to do without the father, without utilizing him, ends up producing only frustrated attachment filled with rage. Hate impedes separation and becomes a kind of indestructible bond.

The failure of inheritance is the failure in the way of correctly understanding the meaning of the Law of the word, of understanding the knot that unites and does not separate Law and desire, freedom and responsibility. Paternal testimony knows how to keep both the Law of castration and the gift of desire, prohibition and donation. But this union in a time of the father's evaporation is no longer supported by the *automaton* of tradition, by the symbolic power of the Name of the Father. For this reason, our time demands we rethink the paternal function from the top down, as testimony, as an act, as an incarnation of the vital force of desire. Let's take the example of sexuality. There was a time in which sexual and emotional lives within the family were cloaked in moral taboos. The exercise of prohibition extended to the life of drive like the shadow cast by the setting sun. This regrettably disciplinary model has burnt itself out, as happened with the time in which praying was like breathing. Sexuality is no longer anchored down by taboos and moral condemnation. Its education no longer coincides with the rigidly normative idea of correction or, worse still, of eradication. And yet it is precisely the end of this disciplinary discourse that places parents before the responsibility for their action. If it is no longer the big Other of tradition that exerts control over the sexual body, that includes it in a discourse of value, if so-called sexual education is no longer ensured by the invasiveness of moralistic regulations, how should we behave when faced with the sexual curiosity, behaviour and practices of our children? This problem does not empty the educational discourse but inevitably fills it with new content and new responsibilities.

## Act, Faith and Promise

How does the transmission of desire take place from one generation to the next? Through a testimony embodied by how one can live with desire. The gift of testimony is the gift of the Other that makes inheritance possible. An encounter with a testimony of this kind is necessary in order for a transmission of desire, and therefore symbolic filiation, to take place. But what is a testimony that makes the gift of desire possible? I would like to sum it up in three words: *act, faith and promise.*

What is the act in the process of symbolic filiation? It is testimony as the embodiment of the Word. There is no testimony unless there is an act. What we need today is an embodiment of testimony as that which is capable of bringing into existence the possibility of desire and its transmission. There is no need for pedagogical rhetoric or moral preaching, no need for edifying sermons. If no professional witnesses exist, or rather, if the professional witnesses are an obstacle to the act of testimony,[17] we must highlight the contingent value of testimony as an encounter. This encounter does not necessarily occur in family relationships. There is testimony wherever there is an encounter with an incarnation of the Law of desire. This is what happens to Totò, the young protagonist in Giuseppe Tornatore's film *Cinema Paradiso*. He finds in a provincial projectionist (Alfredo, played by Philippe Noiret) the witness of an intense, irreducible passion for cinema. This passion will go on to constitute the invisible gift that is transmitted in the chain of generations, but only after the tragic fire that will cost his teacher his sight. It is only when castration besieges the place of the father that he can give testimony of desire and, as a consequence, make symbolic filiation possible. Here the myth of Oedipus is positively overturned, making inheritance possible: the 'child' becomes a famous director, his gaze will be capable of seeing and letting the spectators see other worlds because the 'father's' gaze has renounced being able to see anything at all, because he has testified to his own desire through the cessation of a quota of his libidinal drive. It is no coincidence that the inheritance acquired at the moment of the elderly adoptive father's death will be a film composed of all the fragments of films that the moralistic censorship carried out by the village priest (Father Adelfio) had forbidden from being shown on screen. Whilst the moralistic version of the Law censures Eros, the Law of the word is the Law of desire that leaves as an inheritance the passion of the kiss, the powerful force of love that no censor can ever dream of blocking out. In this film composed of scraps, of remains that have survived, inheritance assumes the force of the Law of desire.

What is *faith*? It is the most profound gift of parenthood. It means believing unreservedly and without self-interest in the desire of one's own children. To have faith in one's children is to sustain the generative power of the desire of the Other. It is to confidently believe in the visions, plans and strength of one's own children. This faith feeds desire because the faith of the Other, of the Other's desire, is that which feeds the faith of the child themselves in their own desire. If the child's desire is viewed with anxiety or suspicion it is not effectively nourished. However, if desire is not a whim, it must prove its constancy, its tenacity, its insistence. The Law of desire is not just a flash in the pan. It demands to be put to the test. Its call must not just be heard, it must also be cultivated over time. Faith in children completes the gesture of prohibition. If faith does not integrate the Law of castration, this Law will appear as nothing more than a senseless, inhuman weight. In order to free the Law from the Law, in order to complete the Law, an act of faith is required, as an act can never be founded on a guarantee, but is always exposed to the unknown, and the risk of failure.[18]

What is *promise*? Promise is the existence of a satisfaction that differs from that of deadly enjoyment. Promise is that this other satisfaction may be greater, richer, stronger, more vital than that offered by deadly enjoyment. Promise is that only if deadly enjoyment is refused, only if this enjoyment is submitted to the Law of castration, will there be access to an enjoyment that is not detached from desire, and this *enjoyment that is Other* than deadly enjoyment will be a new force.[19]

The promise of an Other enjoyment, another satisfaction, exists, and it is the task of the older generations to transmit this possibility to the new. The defence of desire implies the defence of this promise. The promise made by parents is a promise that there will be a life capable of providing human satisfaction. It is the promise of resurrection on Earth. But what is a life risen within life? Are adults capable, like Odysseus, of sustaining the promise of the existence of an Other enjoyment, another satisfaction? Promise is keeping a horizon on the world open. It is earning the world, making of the world that which it is not yet. There is a Christian matrix to which I refer in these thoughts on promise: it is necessary to die of deadly enjoyment, it is necessary to die of enjoyment without hope of the death drive, in order to be able to be born again, to rise to a new life, a life of desire and Other enjoyment. It requires life being given up to the wilderness, so that it might reclaim itself as human. Also, we do not have a movement of appropriation here: the liberation from deadly enjoyment implies exposing oneself, defenceless, to the contingent power of the desire of the Other.

# Epilogue

## *Reading Pain On the Leaves*

As a child I had two heroes: Jesus and Telemachus. It was my way of meditating on the bond with *my* father and his *absence*. I was raised in a family too busy working to take care of their own children. My analysis freed me from vengeful torment, leading me to discover a structural fact within this absence: being a father is always being an absence. Is this not what Jesus and Telemachus both traumatically experienced? Are Jesus and Telemachus not two sons who have profoundly known the father's abandonment, his most radical absence?

If the father is an absence, or rather if his absence is always present,[1] he cannot help but leave us orphans. To be children, to be heirs, always means also being orphaned. The rightful heir does not plug the truth of the structure, does not cancel out the fact that no father will be able to save us. But if the Name of the Father is this absence, this void, it is impossible to fill, the act of the real father (of a parent) makes a transmission possible and provides the foundations for the symbolic filiation that can humanize life. This act is the contingent encounter with a testimony, with a singular incarnation of the Law of desire. In fact, there is only a father where there is the singular testimony of how it is possible to keep together, and not oppose, Law and desire. Only where the name of the Law is not the name of an oppression, but a liberation. Anything can be a father; anything can make possible the encounter with the new alliance between Law and desire. Anything can return from the sea. A Bible-reading boxing coach, like Frankie in Clint Eastwood's *Million Dollar Baby*, an ageing pensioner, a primary school teacher, a mother, the reading of a literary classic, a work of art, a mayor, a film fan ... Inheritance is never a blood inheritance, it is not the consolidation of a solid identity. That which is inherited is always *a testimony*. As such, every paternity, as Françoise Dolto explained, is radically adoptive.[2] All of Clint Eastwood's recent films exalt the possibility of the transmission of desire beyond blood or natural ties.[3] What is the point that we still need to underline? It is that anything, any contingent encounter, can carry with it the gift of the possible testimony of the alliance between Law and desire. Professional witnesses do not exist, and neither does a pedagogy of testimony. It can only be recognized retroactively. If the testimony must be emancipated from every exemplary ideal, it must also be liberated from every form of programming. It exists in the time of pure contingency. It does not respond to a plan, it cannot be ensured, it does not depend upon a technician. The strength of testimony lies in its occurrence there where you would least expect it. It is not an intention but an event that we can only truly reconstruct retroactively. I will only be able to say what a testimony has been for me once I have moved beyond the time in which I experienced it.

I would like to give two biographical examples. The first involves my mother. In the most fiery days of my youth I violently ruptured my relationship with school in order to dedicate myself fully to political militancy. It was the end of the 1970s. Going to school seemed to me and many of my school friends to be a waste of time. We had the movement, and the world to change. Everything that was being said to us seemed dead in the water. Politics, however, was joy, a reason for living; an experience of the resurrection of desire. Faced with the umpteenth failure of my school year, I had no more reason to hesitate. I saw my relationship with the school as over. But I had neglected the fact I was a child, I had neglected my mother's word. A few months after my decision, she waited for me by our front door. She had been too poor to study, and had difficulty writing correctly in Italian due to the profound influence the Friulian dialect of her origins still had on her use of the language. At the door she simply said to me that I should continue my studies. 'Why?' I asked her abruptly, 'That school means nothing to me!', I said, thinking that would put an end to that brief conversation. 'Because it's what everyone does', she responded with disarming force. 'Don't be like me, you have a choice. If you study you won't regret it.' Her conclusion showed no originality. What was she telling me if not that if I had continued to study, I would have seen more things, more lives, more worlds than those she had been able to see, not having had the opportunity? She wanted to tell me not to close myself in my world, not to abandon the world's stage, to stay in the world. Hers was for me, retroactively, a testimony in the

144

strongest sense of the word. Her word had been a promise: 'If you give up closing yourself in your world, if you give up the violence of your world, if you focus on your studies, you will discover other worlds you didn't even know existed! You will be able to open new worlds, to earn other worlds!' This is what happened over time. In this way, my mother's promise became a testimony.

The second episode involves my father. I remember him walking in long strides ahead of me on Sunday mornings, as we went to visit the greenhouse benches on which his ill plants were painfully dying. His uncertain Italian marked by dialect mysteriously gave way to Latin. In that ancient and unknown language he would pronounce the names of the illnesses and those of his plants. He read their pain on their leaves, which had been bitten by invisible insects with the most mysterious names or invaded by mould and spectral speckles, and then prepared magic potions for the treatments that would cure them. He had made all of this from nothing. He had accepted the meagre material inheritance from his own father – who had a certain passion for working the land but preferred to indulge himself among his humble antiques – and made it flourish in an unexpected way. He had invented a profession, that of a florist, without there having been any family precedent.

In my clinical work I have always had a passion for the dimension of the differential diagnosis, for identifying the particular subjective structure that guides the subject's discourse. Where did this passion come from? The childhood memory of my father dedicated to the pain of the leaves contains the core of my inheritance. What did I inherit? I did not inherit a kingdom or an illustrious descendence, no genes nor any wealth, but a silent testimony of desire. I would watch my father bent over his plants. And I knew that was his life, that was his work, that was his satisfaction, his world. To take that pain from the plants, to give them their lives back, to make them grow strong. To save them from mould, from evil, from extra-terrestrial colonies of invisible insects. To dedicate himself to reading and curing the leaves. And what have I become? Am I not someone who also reads the pain on the leaves? Who reads people as if they were leaves? Is this not what I have become? Someone who attempts to read and to cure the pain written on the leaves of the *human humus?* Inheritance is always the inheritance of a passion that is diverted, twisted, deviated somehow. Reading the pain on the leaves: I realized that I have done nothing more than continue doing this, albeit in an entirely different way. This is what it means to inherit: to discover I have become that which I had always been, to make my own – to reclaim – that which had always been mine.

Telemachus was right: something always returns from the sea.

# Notes

## Introduction

1 Eugenio Scalfari, *La Repubblica*, 27 December 1998.

2 Mario Perrotta, 'Odyssey', in *Eredi* [*Heirs*], ed. Federico Condello, Bononia University Press, Bologna 2011, pp. 74–105.

3 See Luigi Zoja, *Il gesto di Ettore: Preistoria, storia, attualità e scomparsa del padre* [*Hector's Gesture: Pre-History, History, Modernity and the Disappearance of the Father*], Bollati Boringhieri, Turin 2000, p. 305.

4 'The father is always at the heart of Telemachus. In no other ancient or classical Greek work is the bond between a son and his father represented with the same sensitivity.' See G. Aurelio Privitera, *Il ritorno del guerriero: Lettura dell'Odissea* [*The Warrior's Return: A Reading of the Odyssey*], Einaudi, Turin 2005, p. 64.

5 (Translator's note: This was part of a student demonstration held in Rome in 2010, protesting the perceived attack on culture, literature and thought in public life. The so-called 'book-shields' were replicated in demonstrations in other capital cities.)

6 *Human humus* is a Lacanian coinage, which he uses to allude to the very problem of transmitting desire as an essential fertilizer of

human life: 'The knowledge designated by Freud as the unconscious is what the human humus invents in order to live on, in one generation and the next.' Jacques Lacan, *Note italienne* [*Italian Note*], in *Autres écrits* [*Other Writings*], Seuil, Paris 2001, p. 311.

## Chapter 1   The Law of the Word and the New Hell

1   Massimo Recalcati, *Cosa resta del padre? La paternità nell'epoca ipermoderna* [*What Remains of the Father? Fatherhood in the Hypermodern Age*], Raffaello Cortina, Milan 2011.

2   See Jacques Lacan, 'Note on the Father and Universalism', *Lacanian Review*, 3 (Spring 2017), p. 11. See also Massimo Recalcati, *L'uomo senza inconscio: Figure della nuova clinia psicoanalista* [*Man Without Unconscious: Figures in New Psychoanalytic Treatment*], Raffaello Cortina, Milan 2010, pp. 3–69, and *Cosa resta del padre?*

3   I would like to point out that it is precisely with the symptom of aphasia that Freud begins his clinical research. We must never forget that the practice of psychoanalysis, which is a putting into practice of the word, is born from an interrogation into what makes the word impossible.

4   This point is made by Antonio Tricomi in his excellent book on Pasolini's opus: 'The logic of squander is no longer a practical alternative in an age of triumphalist neo-capitalism. While, for example, Bataille had been able to believe in the need to recognize the incredible transgressive value of filth, now Pasolini is forced to recognize that it is also a tool of Power: those who produce force consumers to eat shit.' Antonio Tricomi, *Sull'opera mancata*

*di Pasolini: Un autore irrisolto e il suo laboratorio* [*On Pasolini's Missing Work: An Unresolved Author and his Laboratory*], Carocci, Rome 2005, p. 421.

5 Cesare Musatti, 'Il *Salò* di Pasolini regno della perversione' ['Pasolini's *Salò*, Reign of Perversion'], *Cinema Nuovo*, 239 (January–February 1976).

6 The critical importance of this attempt does not escape Gian Carlo Ferretti, as we see in his book *Pasolini: L'universo orrendo* [*Pasolini: The Horrendous Universe*], Editori Riuniti, Rome 1976, pp. 106–10. On the Lacanian concept of the capitalist discourse, see Recalcati, *L'uomo senza inconscio*, particularly the first part.

7 Citation from Tricomi, *Sull'opera mancata di Pasolini*, p. 417. For Lacan, see Jacques Lacan, 'Kant with Sade', in *Écrits* [*Writings*], trans. Bruce Fink, W. W. Norton, New York 2006, pp. 645–70.

8 Here, the villa in Salò calls to mind (albeit in a much more farcical, though no less tragic, way) Silvio Berlusconi's villa at Arcore during its more 'glorious' years. In both cases we are faced not so much with the perverse fantasy of its protagonists (whose sexual fantasy is not perverse?) or the erotic dimension of desire as with the terror of the 'master' when having to confront the testing of his own limits, with the collapse of the illusion of his own fantasy of self-generation, with the impending immanence of his own death. We therefore have a defacing of the Ideal, the reduction of every Ideal to pure semblance, in order to assert that the only eternal thing, the only Thing that counts, the only Law capable of forestalling the inevitability of death, is the 'will to enjoyment'.

9 For an overview of this subject, see Massimo Recalcati, 'Desiderio, godimento e soggettivazione' ['Desire, Enjoyment

and Subjectivization'], in *Jacques Lacan*, Raffaello Cortina, Milan 2012.

10  See Collette Soler, *L'epoca dei traumi/L'Époque des traumatismes* [*The Era of Trauma*], Biblink editori, Rome 2004 (bilingual).

11  See Jacques Lacan, *Le Séminaire. Livre XVIII: D'un discours qui ne serait pas du semblant* [*The Seminar. Book XVIII: On a Discourse That Would Not Be the Semblance*], Seuil, Paris 2011.

12  This negation of the impossible finds its most heart-rending, perhaps most desperate expression in the Anti-Oedipal culture formalized in a philosophically accomplished way by Gilles Deleuze and Félix Guattari in *Anti-Oedipus: Capitalism and Schizophrenia*, Continuum, London 2009.

13  Lucretius, *De Rerum Natura*, trans. Richard Jenkyns, Penguin, Harmondsworth 2007, p. 178 (V. 961).

14  This point is insisted upon with particular force by the theology of Bultmann, in his powerful interpretation of the madness of Nazism and the phenomenon of totalitarianism more generally. Every anthropocentric vision of the world risks feeding this madness; the greatest sin committed by the human creature, its greatest arrogance, is to misrecognize the symbolic debt that binds life to the Other, to believe oneself free from debt and narcissistically self-generated. See in particular Rudolf Bultmann, *This World and Beyond: Marlburg Sermons*, Scribner, New York 1960.

15  I recall here that, for Lacan, love means 'giving the Other that which one does not have', giving them the sign of our lack.

16  I found this intense example in Jean-Paul Lebrun, *La perversion ordinaire: Vivre ensemble sans autrui* [*The Ordinary Perversion: Living Together Without Others*], Denoël, Paris 2007, pp. 234–5.

17  See Lacan, 'The Subversion of the Subject and the Dialectic of Desire in the Freudian Unconscious', in *Écrits*, p. 698.

18  See Søren Kierkegaard, *Repetition and Philosophical Crumbs*, Oxford University Press, Oxford 2009.

19  This is the extreme point reached by prayer when it becomes an act in itself, as Thomas of Celano recalls occurring to St Francis: 'He prayed no more, he had now become prayer' ('Non tam orans, quam oratio factus'). See Enzo Bianchi, *Why Pray, How To Pray*, St Pauls, London 2015.

20  *Hilflosigkeit* is the word used by Freud to describe the discarded condition, lacking any foundations, of the human existence. In German, *Hilf* means help and *Losigkeit* means loss. Lacan translates this idea with the more poetic expression 'absolute distress'. See Jacques Lacan, *The Seminar of Jacques Lacan. Book X: Anxiety*, Polity, Cambridge 2014, p. 137.

21  Jacques Lacan, *The Seminar of Jacques Lacan. Book XI: The Four Fundamental Concepts of Psychoanalysis* (1964), ed. Jacques-Alain Miller, W. W. Norton, New York 1998, p. 77.

22  Philip Roth, *Nemesis*, Vintage, New York 2010, p. 265. I must thank Federica Manzon for reminding me of this passage.

23  See Albert Camus, *The Plague*, Penguin, Harmondsworth 1989, pp. 78–84, 180–91.

24  Camus, *Plague*, p. 185.

25  See Erich Fromm, *Escape From Freedom*, Ishi Press, New York 2011.

26  On the toxic risks of mass identification I would recommend the peerless book by Eugenio Gaburri and Laura Ambrosiano, *Ululare coi lupi: Conformismo e rêverie* [*Howling with Wolves:*

*Conformism and Reverie*], Bollati Boringhieri, Turin 2003. For more on this subject see also the classic study by Wilhelm Reich, *The Mass Psychology of Fascism*, Souvenir Press, London 1997.

27 Hannah Arendt, *The Origins of Totalitarianism*, Penguin, Harmondsworth 2017.

28 Mark 7: 18–23.

29 On the 'greatest madness' of narcissism, as understood by psychoanalysis, see Recalcati, *Jacques Lacan*, pp. 1–66.

30 Massimo Cacciari, 'Il peso dei padri' ['The Fathers' Burden'], in Enzo Bianchi, Massimo Cacciari, Ivano Dionigi, Paolo Grossi, Massimo Recalcati and Barbara Spinelli, *Eredi: Ripensare i padri* [*Heirs: Rethinking Fathers*], ed. Ivano Dionigi, Rizzoli, Milan 2012, p. 28.

31 This is one of the points furthest from the analysis developed by Mauro Magatti in his important work. See Mauro Magatti, *La libertà immaginaria: Le illusioni del capitalismo tecno-nichilista* [*Imaginary Freedom: The Illusions of Techno-Nihilistic Capitalism*], Feltrinelli, Milan 2009, and *La grande contrazione: I fallimenti della libertà e le vie del suo riscatto* [*The Great Contraction: The Failures of Freedom and the Paths for its Redemption*], Feltrinelli, Milan 2012.

32 See in particular Massimo Recalcati, *Clinica del vuoto: Anoressie, dipendenze, psicosi* [*Treating the Void: Anorexia, Addiction, Psychosis*], FrancoAngeli, Milan 2002, and *L'uomo senza inconscio*.

33 Lucretius, *De Rerum Natura*, p. 196 (VI. 20).

34 For further comment, see Massimo Recalcati, *Ritratti del desiderio* [*Portraits of Desire*], Raffaello Cortina, Milan 2012, pp. 75–86.

35 See Homer, *The Odyssey*, Penguin, Harmondsworth 2003, Book XXI, pp. 277–300. An intense reading of this scene can be found in Zoja's *Il gesto di Ettore*, pp. 117–20.

36 For the young Marx, work manifests the active life of human beings, the human essence of man, because it is only in work, in 'the working-up of the objective world, therefore, that man first really proves himself to be a *species being*. [...], for he duplicates himself not only, as in consciousness, intellectually, but also actively, in reality, and therefore he contemplates himself in a world that he has created'. Karl Marx and Fredrick Engels, *Economic & Philosophic Manuscripts of 1844 and The Communist Manifesto*, Prometheus Books, Amherst 1988, p. 77.

37 Could we not interpret the opposition between work and finance with the categories of desire and enjoyment? Is work not one of the highest expressions of desire? And is the profit made through financial speculation (made by taking the 'shortcut') not a paradigm of deadly enjoyment that refuses the 'long way round' of sublimation?

## Chapter 2  The Confusion Between Generations

1 It was Giacomo Contri who, many years ago now, re-evaluated the crucial importance of this figure as a paradigm for a certain (hypermodern) way of abusing the Law with impunity. See Giacomo Contri, 'Il lavoro di querela' ['The Role of Complaint'], *La Psicoanalisi*, 1 (1987), pp. 178–89.

2 See Homer, *Odyssey*, Book II, pp. 15–16.

3 On the role of family mediation in terms of psychoanalysis, see the pertinent work by Marco Bouchard and Giovanni Mierolo, *Offesa e riparazione: Per una nuova giustizia attraverso la mediazione* [*Offence and Reparation: For a New Justice Through Mediation*], Bruno Mondadori, Milan 2005.

4 Marcel Gauchet, *Il figlio del desiderio: Una rivoluzione antropologica* [*The Child of Desire: An Anthropological Revolution*], Vita e Pensiero, Milan 2010.

5 See Lebrun, *La perversion ordinaire*.

6 Marilynne Robinson, *Gilead*, Virago, London 2005, p. 147. I would like to thank Aurelio Mottola for having given me this book.

7 See *Avons-nous encore besoin d'un tiers?* [*Do We Still Need A Third?*], ed. Jean-Pierre Lebrun and Elisabeth Volckrick, Érès, Toulouse 2005.

8 See Massimo Recalcati, *L'omogeneo e il suo rovescio: Per una clinica psicoanalitica del piccolo gruppo monosintomatico* [*The Homogenous and its Reverse: For a Psychoanalytic Treatment of Small Monosymptomatic Groups*], FrancoAngeli, Milan 2005.

9 Before we entrusted ourselves to the so-called 'technocrats', the Lega (Northern League) had found in mythology – that of the sources of the River Po and the ideal of the Padanian lands – the way to subtract politics from its technocratic evaporation. Today's new populism confirms the total irrationality of myth by leaning on the technological democracy guaranteed by the Internet in order to avoid the 'swindle' of political mediation. But both these options – that of myth and that of technological democracy – appear to be profoundly narcissistic because they

are incapable of understanding that politics is precisely the art of mediation, the continual exercise of translation.

10 The invocation of direct democracy, which reacts in an anti-institutional way to the unbearable weakness and degeneration of institutions, risks raising from the dead a populism that ends up throwing the baby away with the bathwater of democracy. *Grillismo* (Translator's note: named after the founder of the Five Star Movement, comedian Beppe Grillo) boasts a form of direct democracy for the citizen that refuses any kind of mediation, and, as such, views the social function of political parties as old hat. The signs of discord that run through this movement do not, however, augur anything positive. It is a film we have already seen. It is a historical and psychological law, both collective and individual: whoever places themselves outside the system of political debate and the exercise of symbolic mediation imposed by democracy ends up creating the same monster they are, rightly, fighting against.

11 (Translator's note: Francesco Schettino was the captain of the *Costa Concordia*, which sank off the coast of Capri in January 2012. Schettino is believed to have caused the tragedy in which thirty-two people died by crashing into rocks whilst trying to impress his lover who was on the bridge with him, in an alleged attempt to make the ship 'bow' to the island on its approach. He then proceeded to abandon ship before many of the passengers had been moved to safety. His conversation with Captain Gregorio De Falco of the Italian Coastguard (referred to later on) is now infamous, with his furious colleague ordering him to return to the ship, as his position dictates, and Schettino stubbornly refusing.)

12 See Francesco Cataluccio, *Immaturità: La malattia del nostro tempo*, [*Immaturity: The Disease of Our Time*], Einaudi, Turin 2004.

13 (Translator's note: Literally 'big children'; this word denotes someone who, despite having reached the age of maturity, continues to behave in an irresponsible, infantile manner, choosing to depend on their parents for everything.)

14 See Giovanni Bottiroli, 'Non sorvegliati e impuniti: Sulla funzione sociale dell'indisciplina' ['Unwatched and Unpunished: The Social Function of Indiscipline'], in *Forme contemporanee del totalitarismo* [*Contemporary Forms of Totalitarianism*], ed. Massimo Recalcati, Bollati Boringhieri, Turin 2007, pp. 118–40.

15 Does the cavalier use of public money by our politicians, even for the most ephemeral and laughable personal expenses (finally investigated and pursued by the Law), not remind us of the superficiality of certain adolescents who waste their parents' hard-earned money without the slightest sense of guilt, safe in the belief they are entitled to everything? An even more eloquent paradox is when it is the adolescent children themselves – *as adolescent children* – who are given institutional roles through no personal merit (as is the well-known case of the son of Umberto Bossi, known, à propos of the alteration of processes in symbolic filiation, as 'Trota' or the trout). It is certainly in no way coincidental that the dimension of guilt and shame in our time has almost entirely disappeared from the political and social scene.

16 The thesis on the non-existence of the sexual relationship is of the utmost importance for Lacan. For a broader explanation of

this aphorism, whose complexity cannot be reduced, and to more rigorously contextualize all of the themes discussed here, see Recalcati, *Jacques Lacan*, pp. 467–549.

17 The cynicism of this new world was recently described with lucid ruthlessness by Walter Siti, in his novel *Resistere non serve a niente* [*Resistance is Futile*], Rizzoli, Milan 2012. This book can also be read as a more general reflection on the theme of the body of drive in the era of the nihilistic and neo-capitalist extinction of the ideal of love.

18 Mauro Grimoldi, *Adolescenze estreme: I perché dei ragazzi che uccidono* [*Extreme Adolescence: Why Young Men Kill*], Feltrinelli, Milan 2006.

19 Adriano Sofri, 'La Spoon River delle donne' ['Woman's Spoon River'], *La Repubblica*, 3 May 2012.

20 Theodor W. Adorno and Max Horkheimer, *Dialectic of Enlightenment*, Stanford University Press, Stanford 2007, pp. 137–72.

21 See Jacques Lacan, 'Lo stordito', *Scilicet*, 4 (1977), p. 366. For the French original see 'L'etourdit', *Scilicet*, 4 (1973), pp. 5–52.

22 Little Ernst, left alone by his mother, invents a game precisely because of this maternal absence; a game that consists of throwing a spool with thread wrapped around it as far from his sight as possible (*Fort*) before then making it reappear (*Da*). In this game, the child repeats the experience of separation from his mother in a playful symbolization. The spool is, therefore, an object elevated to the dignity of the subject on the background of the mother's absence. See Sigmund Freud, *Beyond the Pleasure Principle and Other Writings*, Penguin, Harmondsworth 2003, pp. 52–5.

23 See Mario Giorgetti Fumel, *Legami virtuali. Internet: Dipendenza o soluzione?* [*Virtual Bonds. Internet: Addiction or Solution?*], Di Girolamo, Trapani 2010, and *Abitanti della rete: Giovani, relazioni e affetti nell'epoca digitale* [*Inhabitants of the Internet: Young People, Relationships and Affections in the Digital Age*], ed. Chiara Giaccardi, Vita e Pensiero, Milan 2010.

24 Aldo Becce, speech given at the conference 'New Technologies: Opportunities for Communication and Risk of Social Isolation', Bologna, 19 March 2011.

25 Sigmund Freud, 'Leonardo Da Vinci: A Memory of his Childhood', in *The Complete Psychological Works of Sigmund Freud. Vols. 1–24*, W.W. Norton, New York 1976, vol. XII, p. 2294.

26 See Sigmund Freud, 'Some Additional Notes on Dream Interpretation as a Whole', in *Complete Psychological Works*, vol. XIX, pp. 4049–52.

27 See Sigmund Freud, 'Some Reflections on Schoolboy Psychology', in *Complete Psychological Works*, vol. XIII, p. 2875.

## Chapter 3   From Oedipus to Telemachus

1 Despite the merciless violence of the authors of *Anti-Oedipus*, psychoanalysts should read and re-read their work again today as a great breath of fresh air. Beneath the revolutionary rhetoric of the liberation of the schizo-body, beyond the law of the 'body without organs' as a pure desiring-machine, as a factory of drive-led enjoyment, this book contains a series of critiques of psychoanalysis that cannot be easily ignored. For example, there is

that of the paranoid and violent use of interpretation (if a patient says *x* this means *y*); that of the unconscious as a family theatre, closed in on itself, that would lose sight of its social character and its infinite collective connections; that of the conformist and moralistic apology of the reality principle and adaptation as the ultimate aim of analytic practice; that of an entirely political use of money that selects patients on the basis of their income; that of the valorization of the Ego and its performance principle. The list could easily, and usefully, go on.

2  Deleuze and Guattari, *Anti-Oedipus*, p. 1.

3  'One is always responsible for one's position as a subject.' Lacan, 'Science and Truth', in *Écrits*, p. 729.

4  For more on these themes I would advise you to see Massimo Recalcati, *Elogio dell'inconscio: Dodici argomenti in difesa della psicoanalisi* [*In Praise of the Unconscious: Twelve Arguments in Defence of Psychoanalysis*], Bruno Mondadori, Milan 2009.

5  Deleuze and Guattari, *Anti-Oedipus*, p. 31.

6  Gilles Deleuze and Félix Guattari, *A Thousand Plateaus: Capitalism and Schizophrenia*, University of Minnesota Press, Minneapolis 1987, p. 228.

7  Deleuze and Guattari, *Thousand Plateaus*, p. 229.

8  Gilles Lipovetsky, *L'ère du vide: Essai sur l'individualisme contemporain* [*The Age of Emptiness: An Essay on Contemporary Individualism*], Gallimard, Paris 1983, and *Hypermodern Times: Themes for the 21st Century*, Polity, Cambridge 2005; Gustavo Pietropolli Charmet, *I nuovi adolescenti: Padri e madri di fronte a una sfida* [*The New Adolescents: Fathers and Mothers Facing a Challenge*], Raffaello Cortina, Milan 2000, and, in particular,

*Fragile e spavaldo: Ritratto dell'adolescente di oggi* [*Fragile and Arrogant: A Portrait of Today's Adolescents*], Laterza, Bari 2008.

9  In psychoanalytic treatment, the absence of a guilty conscience defines in a strict sense the position of the perverse subject. See Lacan, 'Kant with Sade', in *Écrits*.

10  Pietropolli Charmet, *Fragile e spavaldo*, p. 63.

11  See Francesco Stoppa, *La restituzione: Perché si è rotto il patto tra le generazioni* [*The Restitution: Why the Generational Pact has Broken*], Feltrinelli, Milan 2011, pp. 121–33; Catherine Ternynck, *L'uomo di sabbia: Individualismo e perdita di sé* [*The Man of Sand: Why Individualism Makes Us Sick*], Vita e Pensiero, Milan 2012, pp. 53–73. For the French original, see Catherine Ternynck, *L'homme du sable: Pourquoi l'individualisme nous rends malades*, Seuil, Paris 2011.

12  Homer, *Odyssey*, Book XVI, p. 213.

13  Odysseus is not only the image of the cunning of bourgeois reason, as Adorno and Horkheimer want to demonstrate in *Dialectic of Enlightenment*. He does not limit himself to evading the imposition of sacrifice in order to reach an enjoyment that lies outside the Law, but he is also the one who knows how to refuse deadly enjoyment in order to stay faithful to his desire (to return to Penelope) and his paternal promise (to return to Telemachus). We know how the myth tells us that Odysseus had no desire to leave for the long Trojan War, and in order to convince him to go, the head of little Telemachus is placed beneath the sharpened ploughshare. In that moment, he has no doubts about sacrificing his life and liberty for those of his son. The same thing will happen in his vicissitudes at sea. No encounter, no fate will ever

completely distract him from his task of returning, from his limit-less responsibility to his family.

14  See Recalcati, *Ritratti del desiderio*, pp. 116–26.

15  'The Proci have overturned every Law; rather than bringing gifts to the queen they were courting, they guzzled Odysseus' riches. They were guilty of abusing their power, of *hubris*: they exceeded the limits inside which they had been placed by luck and life. They had done away with borders. They had invaded the house of the king, they squandered his wealth, they abused his serving maids, they harassed his wife, they threatened his son's life, they imposed their will on the bard, they incited the servants, they attacked guests and strangers … The poet makes them trample the laws of hospitality, a cornerstone of Greek society. They thus offend Zeus, the host.' Privitera, *Il ritorno del guerriero*, pp. 236–8.

16  See Recalcati, *Ritratti del desiderio*, pp. 119–26.

17  See Jacques Lacan, *The Seminar of Jacques Lacan. Book XX: On Feminine Sexuality, the Limits of Love and Knowledge*, W. W. Norton, New York 1999, p. 108.

18  See Giuseppe Lentini, *Il 'padre di Telemaco': Odisseo tra Iliade e Odissea* [*Telemachus' Father: Odysseus between the Iliad and the Odyssey*], Giardini, Pisa 2006.

19  Homer, *Odyssey*, Book V, p. 68.

20  See Emmanuel Lévinas, *Totality and Infinity: An Essay on Exteriority*, Martinus Nijhoff, Dordrecht 1979.

21  Adorno and Horkheimer, *Dialectic of Enlightenment*, p. 45.

Chapter 4  What Does It Mean To Be a Rightful Heir?

1  Sigmund Freud, 'An Outline of Psychoanalysis', in *Complete Psychological Works*, vol. XIII, p. 5012.

2  This is a theme developed by Philip Roth in *Patrimony: A True Story*, Vintage, New York 2016. See also Recalcati, *Cosa resta del padre?*, pp. 119–53. But should we not perhaps ask ourselves, more radically, whether inheritance is not always made of shit, in the sense that it is only as orphans, as lacking beings, as lives thrown into language, that inheritance becomes possible? Nonetheless, as Roth masterfully shows in the key scene in *Patrimony*, as heirs we must work on this very shit, undertaking a labour of 'secretly' clearing it up, working with that which comes from the father, a labour of impossible care to be taken to its end point once and for all. I owe this reference to the importance of the gesture of 'cleaning' the 'patrimony' left by the father to Girolamo Dal Maso (p.c.).

3  Matthew 8: 18–22.

4  Luke 9: 62.

5  Sigmund Freud, 'Mourning and Melancholia', in *The Standard Edition of the Complete Psychological Works of Sigmund Freud. Book XIV (1914–1916): On the History of the Psychoanalytic Movement, Papers on Metapsychology and Other Works*, Vintage, New York 2001, p. 244.

6  Friedrich Nietzsche, *Untimely Meditations*, Cambridge University Press, Cambridge 1999.

7  Matthew 10: 34.

8  Matthew 12: 48.

9 Franz Kline, 'L'artista è oggi pro o contro il passato?' ['Is Today's Artist For or Against the Past?'], interview by Thomas B. Hess, in Carolyn Christov-Bakargiev and David Anfam, *Franz Kline 1910–1962*, Skira, Milan 2004.

10 Mark 12: 7–8.

11 It is no coincidence that this reminds us how the psychoanalytic treatment of psychotic adolescents frequently intercepts the nexus between the foreclosure of the father's symbolic function and the passage to the parricidal act. It is as if a fantasy of self-generation imposes itself on the backdrop of a negative inheritance, a fantasy of the subject's impossibility of recognizing the symbolic debt it owes the Name of the Father. See François Marty, *Filiation, parricide et psychose à l'adolescence: Les liens du sang* [*Filiation, Parricide and Adolescent Psychosis: The Blood Ties*], Érès, Toulouse 1999.

12 See Cacciari, 'Il peso dei padri'.

13 'And Telemachus flung his arms round his noble father's neck and burst into tears. And now a passionate longing for tears arose in them both and they cried aloud piercingly and more convulsively than birds of prey, vultures or crooked-clawed eagles, bereaved when villagers have robbed the nest of their fledgling young.' See Homer, *Odyssey*, Book XVI, p. 215.

14 In the 'Telemachia' that opens James Joyce's *Ulysses* we find a radical version of the heir as a heretic, the heir created not by himself but by his own Works. Stephen Dedalus is a Telemachus who, unlike Homer's character, would like to definitively renounce all fathers ('Enough of fathers!'). He transforms, through tremendous effort, his impossible inheritance into a

rightful heresy. For an interpretation of inheritance as heresy in the Joycean 'Telemachia', starting with the Lacanian reading of Joyce, see Recalcati, 'Desiderio, godimento e soggettivazione', pp. 219–38.

15 The monumental work Sartre dedicates to Gustave Flaubert can be read as an extraordinary reflection on the subject of inheritance. Gustave can paradoxically be the heir of the Other precisely because of his exclusion by the Other, unlike his older brother, Achille, the firstborn, who is destined to be a literal clone of his father Achille Flaubert, to the point of sharing his very name. There is no way out: the totalizing identification with the heir impedes the singular movement of the reclamation of inheritance. See Jean-Paul Sartre, *The Family Idiot: Gustave Flaubert, 1821–1857. Vol. 2*, University of Chicago Press, Chicago 1991. For further comment on this text and its themes, see Recalcati, *Jacques Lacan*, pp. 424–66.

16 Recalcati, *Clinica del vuoto*, pp. 111–19.

17 It is no coincidence that Roth's portrayal of his protagonist in *Nemesis* is the portrayal of a professional witness who, as such, discovers himself, in a tragic and cruel twist of fate, to be the source of the very evil (polio) he wants to combat.

18 For more on the inevitability and fecund importance of failure along the educational path, see Recalcati, *Elogio del fallimento*.

19 The Law of castration neither prohibits nor abolishes enjoyment, but makes it vital. However, not all enjoyment takes the opportunity offered by the Law, which always leaves a trace of refractory enjoyment in symbolic castration.

## Epilogue

1 See Roberto Esposito, 'Una comunità senza padre' ['A Community Without Fathers'], in *Il padre: Annali del diparti-mento clinico 'G. Lemoine'* [*The Father: Annals of the 'G. Lemoine' Clinical Department*], ed. Francesco Giglio, Et Al., Milan 2013.

2 Her model from the Gospels is St Joseph, who 'submits himself to this imposition, even though the child is not a child of his flesh ... The roles of father and biological parent are often confused. A man requires only three seconds to become a biological parent. Being a father is an entirely different adventure. [...] Perhaps it is better if the father is also the biological parent, but deep down there are only ever adoptive fathers. A father must always adopt their child.' See Françoise Dolto, *I Vangeli alla luce della psico-analisi. La liberazione del desiderio: dialoghi con Gérard Sévérin* [*The Gospels in the Light of Psychoanalysis. The Liberation of Desire: Dialogues with Gérard Sévérin*], Et Al., Milan 2012, p. 14. For the original French, see Françoise Dolto, *L'Evangile au risque de la psychanalyse. Tome 1*, Seuil, Paris 1980.

3 See Recalcati, *Cosa resta del padre?*, pp. 171–89.